Urgent images

Urgen
es:Th
hicla
eofth

timag

egrap

nguag

efax

Booth-Clibborn
Editions

Editor: Edward Booth-Clibborn

Selection edited and project co-ordinated by: Liz Farrelly

Design: Angus Hyland and Silvia Gaspardo Moro

Photography: Ferdy Carabott, Arran Elvidge, Helen McCormack

Reprinted paperback 2000
Paperback edition 1997
Published by Booth-Clibborn Editions 1994

Printed and bound in Hong Kong by Dai Nippon

Thanks, for their kind assistance and creative help, to Clifford Hiscock, Julian Morey, Alan Drew, Vicky Hayward, Derek Husdon at the Science Museum.

Captions and artwork in this book have been supplied by the entrants. While every effort has been made to ensure accuracy, Booth-Clibborn Editions cannot accept responsibility for errors or omissions under any circumstances.

Booth-Clibborn Editions
12 Percy Street
London W1P 9FB

Fax: +44 20 7637 4251

www.booth-clibborn.com

info@booth-clibborn.com

ISBN 1-86154-050-7

Contents

p6. Glitch in a digital world, by Liz Farrelly The last form of hardcopy message in an increasingly computerised world. The history of fax technology and instant message sending. An explanation of why the fax machine is so easily hijacked. A few instances when a simple fax has changed the course of history. The fax aesthetic: Privacy, freedom and discretion.

p18. Dissolution of the mail Faxers explore romantically redundant imagery.

p22. Hardcopy headers Fax stationery: Legible and eye-catching. From the most minimal use of the three-letter word to fax headers that revel in the formal language of documentation. Less formal than a letterhead, potentially the most personal designed statement.

p38. Image net/ omnipresent resolution Designers and illustrators send ideas and images to each other and their clients by fax, around the clock and across continents. Concepts, proofs, final artwork. The aesthetics of fax reproduction, as detected in high-profile projects. Rooting the oeuvre in the technological present.

p72. Technotechnotechno The fax as an image-making device. The range of its mark-making techniques and effects; from photographic quality to the softest monoprint. Designers, artists and students create unique printed pieces, which redefine the term user/machine interface.

p108. Talking zone The fax machine as a symbol of solidarity. Communication between individuals and groups normally excluded from the media and the gallery system. Mass-faxings between educational and cultural institutions.

p140. Metascroll One piece of A4 paper turns into a 30 metre-long scroll covered with information, facts and images.

p164. Error Technology can fail: The results. A reminder of the presence of a machine, intervening and translating our words.

p172. Terminology The jargon: Become an initiate.

Glitc
igita
dbyLi
elly

hinad
lworl
zFarr

Ever since people started daubing pigment onto surfaces artists have been investigating the mark-making potential of various inanimate objects in the quest to translate their imaginations into images and documents. Fuelled by unstoppable invention, the nature of those inanimate objects has constantly changed. Implements were fashioned into tools, tools were refined into instruments, these, when linked to power sources, became machines. More recently, science surpassed itself and formulated technologies, which in turn produced media. Consequently, art and definitions of art also changed. Today, in every field of creativity, artists, designers, architects, film-makers and musicians employ a myriad of technologies, tools, machines, and even a few trusty old implements, in the process of realising their visions.

One of the most potentially creative and therefore frustrating stages in the mark-making process is learning how to use those tools. Some require high levels of skill for dexterous manipulation: paint-brushes, chisels, scissors, Rotring pens. Others require a degree of subversion to transport them out of their allotted parameters of function into another line of duty. This has happened with the printing press and the computer, the humble envelope and the fax machine. The rewards for anyone attempting such re-invention range from accusations of heresy to praise for innovation, depending on the audience. For under the hybrid jungle law of the creative professions, Warhol's "fifteen minutes of fame" drafted on to Darwin's "survival of the fittest", praise/acceptance and infamy/exclusion have become, equally, goals to be aimed for.

Among the tools/implements/machines which especially lend themselves to subversive appropriation - because they are widely available, easy to use and have a potentially large catchment area - is the now omnipresent fax machine. The aim of this book is to demonstrate how it can be hijacked and put to work as a creative device: as part of the design process, as a mark-making implement, and as a means of communicating ideas to whoever is out there. The fax machine has democratised visual communication by making pictures as easy to transmit as words and leaving us open to receiving unsolicited, uncensored material from anywhere on the planet. Able to transmit information - specifications or invoices - around the globe, while also functioning as a personal monoprinter which can add the mark of technology to artwork, the fax machine combines the functionality of a work-horse with the potential of a playtime toy. 1

This collection of images was received in response to a call for entries faxed to around four hundred numbers worldwide. The request became public property and both fax-fans and pranksters responded enthusiastically. The images show how the fax machine has been explored and exploited as more than just a piece of office equipment, principally by designers, but also by writers, artists and students.

The various fax machines we use today range in quality and capability from the most basic version to models that blur the boundaries with computers. Consequently, prices range accordingly, from around £300 up to approximately £20,000 for a full-colour fax, the Canon FO9000, which can only be ordered direct from Japan (UK recommended retail prices). 2 Fortunately, for our purposes, nearly all these machines can talk to each other, thus facilitating communication between all economic levels of the fax-owning population. For although cloaked in high-tech styling, fax technology is relatively simple. This makes the fax machine the perfect tool for infiltrating, broadcasting and mass-producing messages.

Before re-deploying this magical object the happy faxer should know what goes on inside the sleek, usually grey, industrially-designed box when those warbling recognition tones sing out.

In 1843 a Scottish watchmaker, Alexander Bain, formulated a method for "taking copies of surfaces, for instance the surface of printer's types, at distant places". The experiment required that the

message be set in metal type clamped against a frame containing short, parallel wires. These conducted electricity, but only though the wires in contact with the raised type. A swinging pendulum brushed across the frame, creating electrical impulses that were transmitted to another pendulum and wire device, but this time attached to chemically treated paper sensitive to electrical current. As the synchronised pendulums swung, an image of the type was re-drawn by the chemical reaction. Five years later, Frederick Collier Bakewell, working in London, patented a drum-shaped scanner. Marks made with insulating varnish on a flexible metal plate, attached to the spinning drum, could be read and transmitted as electrical impulses and re-drawn by a similar device. In the early years of the twentieth century, American scientist Dr Arther Korn refined the scanning process into a workable office device by developing the "photocell" which enabled ink on paper to be recorded using an electrical current triggered by light.

The basic principles - to scan, transmit, synchronise and output - were developed into manufactured devices, principally for transmitting weather maps and newspaper proofs, and for business use by Xerox in the USA. But they were large, smelly (transmissions were burnt into chemically-treated paper), expensive and could only talk to models produced by the same manufacturer. It wasn't until the manufacturers established international standards, which graded models into separate numbered "Groups", one to four, guaranteeing compatibility, that the commercial world was convinced of the fax machines usefulness. With the setting of these standards in 1974 came the race to develop fax machines that were faster and therefore cheaper to run, compact enough for the desk-top and offering a host of features. Low-cost micro chips and efficient semiconductors have resulted in fax machines that can scan 98 lines per inch, converting each line into 1,728 pixels, which are transmitted at up to 14,400 bits per second in up to 64 tones of grey.

The CCITT standards (Groups one to four) arrived right at the height of Japan's manufacturing boom. Its electronics giants saw in the fax machine a means of speedily converting complex Japanese correspondence into business documents, allowing users to circumvent the intricacies of the Japanese keyboard. Since then handwritten faxed memos have become the standard acceptable means of communicating business documentation in Japan. Fax machines also quickly went domestic. One reason was that the complex method of numbering buildings made a faxed street map, marked with a cross, the easiest way of guaranteeing that your visitor would reach their destination.

The availability of fax machines in Japan has proved a test-bed for experimentation. With the market reaching saturation point, Japanese teenagers have become the latest marketing target, with magazine advertisements showing fax machines pumping out pubescent love letters. As reported in Mediamatic magazine, the combination of a hand-held photocopier and fax, marketed as "The Tokyo Woman's Fax", prompted Alfred Birnbaum and David O'Reilly to pen the strap-line "Anywhere the hand can go, the Fax can go!". They recount how the unsuspecting victim, "Mrs Tacko Hallori (32) received a 25 minute (10 metres) FEX from an unidentified sender during the night...and immediately reported the prank to the police". These sexually explicit faxes are, reportedly, regular invaders of the home and workplace and are now creeping around the world. The question is will the rest of us catch up with Japan's level of fax-dependence, or will computer networking leap-frog the fax machine as the truly modern means of staying in touch?

What advantage has the fax machine over "the net" which can explain why it is the favoured tool of media pranksters? Chance, mystery, distance, speed and an eventual "hardcopy" combine together to make the fax a unique print and communication medium. Coincidentally (?), many inveterate pranksters earn their livings as graphic designers and illustrators. While fulfilling clients' briefs they still find the time, and the inclination, to experiment with the tools of their trade and along the

way cultivate a network of fellow travellers, plus the occasional convert.

As the quality of fax output depends on the capability and specifications of both the faxer's and the faxee's equipment, a degree of chance and doubt is injected into the proceedings. The unfinished honesty of incoming and outgoing faxes have fed into designers' commercial work: a low-resolution fax-patina of blemishes has crept back into images at a time when professional levels of scanning, proofing and printing had almost eradicated the concept of error. Type innovators discovered early on that, with the help of a photocopier and a fax machine they could bend, stretch, fade and bit-map type and images long before the combination of Apple Mac and Adobe made type manipulation easy.

Crucial to the fax-aesthetic is the heat-sensitive thermal paper containing droplets of ink activated by 1,728 tightly-packed heater elements arranged across the width of the paper feeder. The waxy, greyish paper, output from a roll, makes "urgent" faxes easily distinguishable and is vital for experimental work, as it breaks the boundaries of DIN standards and is not simply "blank". Tearing, pulling, scrunching and exposure to sunlight, heat or fire all "activate" marks.

The obsessive quest, by electronics multi-nationals' "Research and Development" departments, to ensure that fax machines catch up with computers is now beginning to put at risk this imperfect, but unique, fax-aesthetic. The "smart" plain-paper fax with a memory, data compression and ECM, which guarantees error-free transmissions, is just one step behind the fax-card, a plug-in circuit board which allows a modem-linked computer to output faxes through a laser printer. When combined with a powerful enough memory, the computer can send and receive homogenised images free of all signs of mechanical mark-making.

But lost glitches won't just be mourned by graphic designers. Over the last decade the fax machine has became a crucial means of disseminating information which, at certain key moments, turned knowledge into power. In 1989 France's _Actuel_ spearheaded an international group of magazines which published, in Chinese, the "Fax for Freedom", along with a list of fax numbers through-out the Peoples Republic. 3 Readers were asked to use the fax to inform the Chinese people of the fate of student demonstrators in Tianamen Square, and warn of the repercussions for human rights of their government's actions. In 1990 the Russian leader Yeltsin sent a declaration of intent by fax to politicians around the world, days before he helped free Gorbachev from kidnappers and moved the Soviet Union another step closer to dissolution. 4

Artists and designers, working both within and outside the gallery and publishing mainstreams, were quick to recognise the democratising nature of the fax machine. David Hockney's media-grabbing use of the fax was the logical outcome of his exploration of new methods of image reproduction, which included making composite photographs with a Polaroid camera and investigating the integrity of "surface" with a colour laser copier. He faxed entire exhibitions to the 1989 Sao Paolo Biennale, to televised events at Salts Mill Gallery in Bradford and later Tokyo. Huge images made from up to 288 A4 sheets were fed into the fax machine at Hockney's studio in Los Angeles, to rematerialise half way around the world and be assembled in front of an eager audience. The critics were surprised at how clear Hockney's faxed drawings and monotone paintings of the Californian seascape were, but as he explained in _That's the way I see it_ (Thames and Hudson, 1993); "There's no such thing as a bad printing machine - so the fax, which is a printing machine, can be used in a beautiful way. To make half-tones, for instance, you don't use washes for something to look like a wash, you use opaque grey; the machine read the opaque greys and made the dots itself. I mixed different greys and so developed quite complicated-looking tones."

An early fax-experimentor, graphic designer Paul Elliman, contemplated sending entire magazines by fax. Travelling aboard, in 1989, he collected visual

evidence of where he'd been, in various media, and faxed it home. Talking to i-D magazine's Jim McClellan, Elliman recounted how; "it was like being in two places at once....it's a kind of four dimensional art". This collection of photographs, comics, calligraphy and handwriting became the prototype for his faxed magazine of images manipulated and collaged by the process of "sending".

A user who understands the capabilities of the fax machine to communicate concepts is American artist Lillian Bell. She responded to a call for entries for this book which was posted on an electronic/computer notice board by Heath Bunting, a multi-media designer in London. Bell has transformed her fax machine into a gallery without walls; "Fax is a new technology for a duty-free and boundary-free art and represents the abolition of time and space." Bell realised that statement at the 1992 Earth Summit in Brazil when she specified, by fax, a built installation for the display of other artists' faxed contributions. By publishing a fax network directory, F'AXis, which includes over 220 artists from 29 countries "who interact by fax", Bell is actively encouraging an alternative method of making and displaying art outside the commercial system of gallery ownership. 5/6/7

Standing outside today's computerised and digitalised global networks, the fax is an interim technology. Intrinsic to its functionality is a basic dichotomy. It exists at the end of a telephone network that has both high and poor quality connections combining digital and analogue technology. The fax machine scans and digitalises the message to be transmitted, but it can't store substantial amounts of information like a computer. The message is therefore both public - anyone passing the receiving machine may read it - but also private, as the original and the output can be destroyed, leaving no trace. It is, in effect, an extension of the oral tradition of telephone conversation and never as static as a piece of typed, proofed, published writing or codified computerised data.

A faxed reminder that no medium is transparent came from another response to the call for entries. Writer and curator Benjamin Weil expressed his hopes for the possibilities of difference being safeguarded through universal communication, aided by the fax machine and the modem; "Words do posit the issue of a global language....English has de facto become the lingua franca (but) in fact, American English, British English or Australian English reflect the particularity of the physical territory they originate from....Similarly, images may be interpreted differently from one side of the planet to the other, or even next door. Adopting a common language might be the most efficient way to relay those cultural differences."

As "SoHo" (Small office Home office) workers are increasingly linked by computerised electronic mail (e-mail) networks so they will use the fax machine less and less. An estimate, stated by Jacques Leslie in Wired magazine, suggests that 16 million business users in the USA send, "the equivalent of 10,000 manuscripts of War and Peace every day of the year" through the e-mail networks. Communication is made easier and instantaneous: no queuing up for the fax machine. But as every one of those messages is traceable - code words can be cracked, and how do you delete e-mail once you've posted it? - surveillance will become a universal by-product of communication. The discretion, privacy and freedom of message sending facilitated by the fax machine is under threat. Maybe, as commerce dispenses with the fax machine, it will be recognised as the only truly undetectable, electronic, spontaneous and global means of sending and receiving what could be crucial messages.

7

1 Sheila de Brettville's faxed specifications. Sent to McCormack, Baron & Associates for a commemorative pavement to be constructed as part of the Ninth Square Public Art Work, 1994.
2 Canon's FO9000 colour fax machine.
3 "Fax for Freedom", published in the UK by <u>The Face</u>, 1989. Reproduced by kind permission of <u>The Face</u>.
4 President Yeltsin's fax, 1990.
5 Lillian Bell's faxed instructions, 1990.
6/7 Catalogues of fax-art projects from Italy and Japan.

СВОДКА НОВОСТЕЙ АГЕНТСТВА "POSTFACTUM" 19/08/91 12.00 1
(С) При использовании информации ссылка на 'POSTFACTUM' обязательна

ОБРАЩЕНИЕ ПРЕЗИДЕНТА РСФСР БОРИСА ЕЛЬЦИНА, ПРЕДСЕДАТЕЛЯ СМ РСФСР ИВАНА СИЛАЕВА, И.О. ПРЕДСЕДАТЕЛЯ ВС РСФСР РУСЛАНА ХАСБУЛАТОВА
К ГРАЖДАНАМ РОССИИ

"В ночь с 18 на 19 августа 1991 года отстранен от власти законно избранный Президент страны.

Какими бы причинами не оправдывалось это отстранение, мы имеем дело с правым, реакционным, антиконституционным переворотом.

При всех трудностях и тяжелейших испытаниях, переживаемых народом, демократический процесс в стране приобретает все более глубокий размах, необратимый характер. Народы России становятся хозяевами своей судьбы. Существенно ограничены бесконтрольные права неконституционных органов, включая партийные. Руководство России заняло решительную позицию по Союзному договору, стремясь к единству Советского Союза, единству России. Наша позиция по этому вопросу позволила существенно ускорить подготовку этого Договора, согласовать его со всеми республиками и определить дату его подписания – 20 августа с.г.

Такое развитие событий вызывало озлобление реакционных сил, толкало их на безответственные, авантюристические попытки решения сложнейших политических и экономических проблем силовыми методами. Ранее уже предпринимались попытки осуществления переворота.

Мы считали и считаем, что такие силовые методы неприемлимы. Они дискредитируют СССР перед всем миром, подрывают наш престиж в мировом сообществе, возвращают нас к эпохе холодной войны и изоляции Советского Союза от мирового сообщества.

Все это заставляет нас объявить незаконным пришедший к власти так называемый комитет. Соответственно, объявляем незаконными [illegible] решения и распоряжения этого комитета.

Уверены, органы местной власти будут неукоснительно [illegible] конституционным Законам и Указам Президента РСФСР.

Призываем граждан России дать достойный ответ путчистам [illegible] требовать вернуть страну к нормальному конституционному развитию.

Безусловно необходимо обеспечить возможность Президенту страны ГОРБАЧЕВУ выступить перед народом. Требуем немедленного созыва Чрезвычайного Съезда народных депутатов СССР.

[illegible] абсолютно уверены, что наши соотечественники не [illegible] утвердиться произволу и беззаконию потерявших всякий стыд и совесть путчистов. Обращаемся к военнослужащим с призывом проявить [illegible] гражданственность и не принимать участие в реакционном перевороте.

До выполнения этих требований призываем к всеобщей бессрочной забастовке.

Не сомневаемся, что мировое сообщество даст объективную [illegible] циничной попытке правого переворота.

19 августа 1991 года, 9.00 утра".

4

2

3

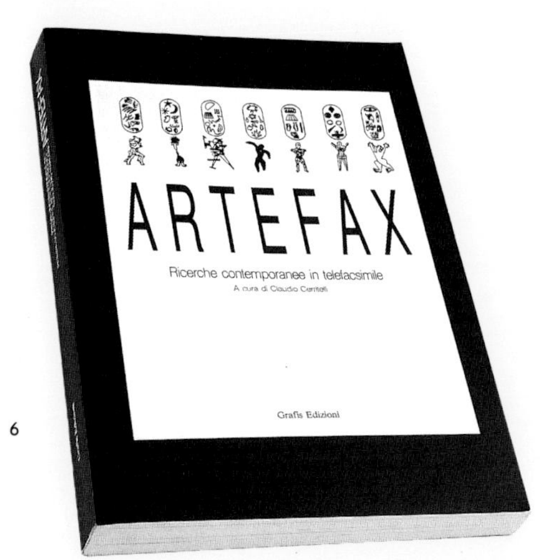
ARTEFAX
Ricerche contemporanee in telefacsimile
A cura di Claudio Cerritelli
Grafis Edizioni

6

Augusta Lewis Troup
typesetter, journalist, activist
Augusta advocated equal pay to women for equal work and organized the internationally recognized Women's Typographical Union No. 1. She edited this newspaper on Center Street, campaigned successfully for public school teachers' pensions, and championed the needs of immigrants and their children.
DAILY UNION
1872

1

TO: FAX 605-688-4973 South Dakota State University, University Program Council Arts & Exhibits Committee
FAX transported Art Exhibition, Box 2815, Brookings, South Dakota 57007-1599, Nov. 1-30,1990
Lillian A. Bell
P.O. Box 1235
McMinnville, OR 97128
Lillian A. Bell
1990
"AT, ON AND UNDER THE TABLE"
Can democracy
survive
manipulation?

5

Disso
lutio
nofth
email

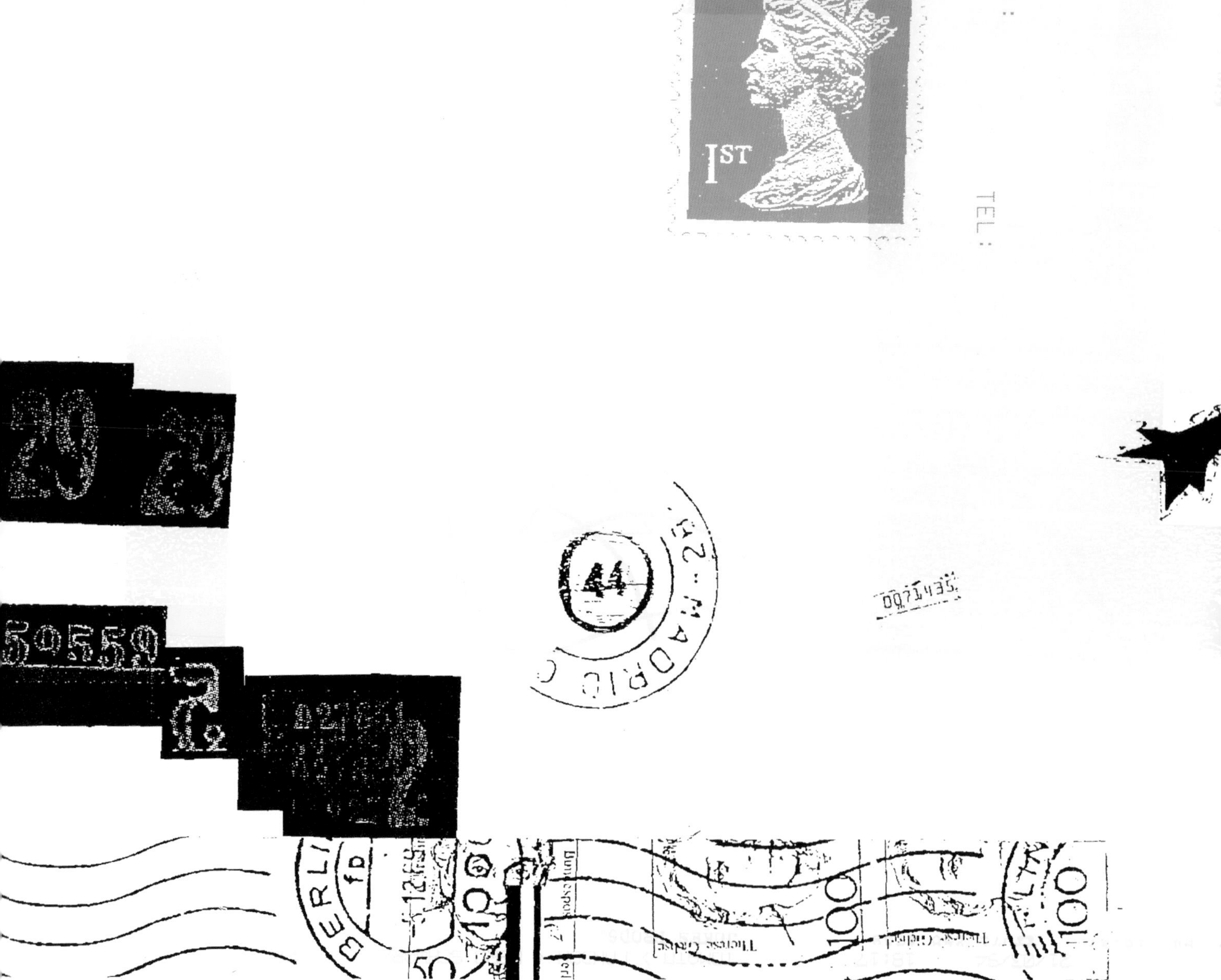

This is an
original piece of
MAIL - ART

Press
andwa
drone

start
itfor
...

Hardc
aders

opyhe

Producing Printed Ephemera for General Consumption.

611 Broadway No. 840
New York, New York 10012

BARRY DECK

GRAPHIC DESIGN
and TYPE DESIGN

FAX!

telephone 212 777 6627
FAX 212 777 6684

FROM

TO

COMPANY

FAX Nº

Nº OF PAGES TO FOLLOW

COMMENTS

THIS IS A FACSIMILE FROM BIG-ACTIVE LIMITED: IF PAGES ARE MISSING OR ILLEGIBLE CALL 071-702 9365.

From

WAREHOUSE D4/RIVERSIDE, METROPOLITAN WHARF, WAPPING WALL,
LONDON E1 9SS. TEL 071-702 9365. FAX 071-702 9366

The J Otto World Company
an illustrator's faxed portfolio
New York
USA

Barry Deck
graphic and typeface designer
New York
USA

Big-Active Limited
graphic designers
London
UK

DOUBLE SPACE

170 Fifth Avenue
New York, NY 10010, USA
Telephone (212) 366 1919
Fax (212) 366 4645

Fax Notice

Date

Number of pages (including this)

From

To

Company

Fax

number

Comments

Please contact our office if there are any problems with transmission. Thank you.

gebr de JONG ontwerpen

Nieuwe Achtergracht 17 1018 XV Amsterdam
telefoon (020)6207895 fax (020)6208368

datum

aan

t.a.v.

#

aantal pag. (incl. dit blad)

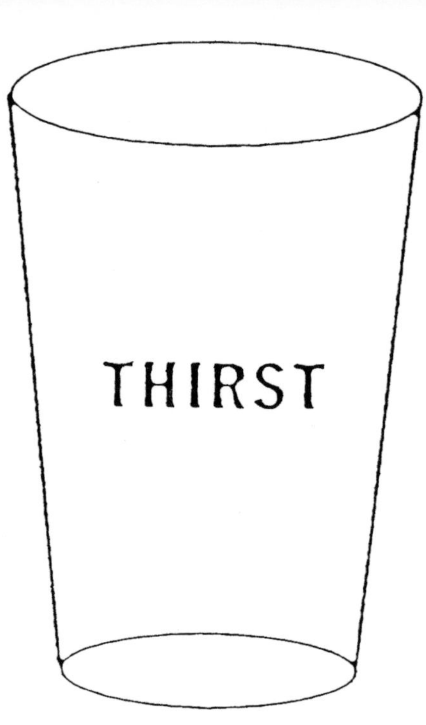

Uden Associates Ltd
Film and Television
Production
Unit 3 Chelsea Wharf
Lots Road
London SW10 0QJ

Tel 071-351 1255/7601
Fax 071-376 3937

Doublespace
design consultancy
New York
USA

gebr de Jong
graphic designers
Amsterdam
The Netherlands

Thirst
Rick Valicenti
graphic designer
Chicago
USA

Uden Associates
Limited
film and television
production company
London
UK

THE INK TANK
FAX MESSAGE

THE INK TANK
FAX MESSAGE

THE INK TANK
FAX MESSAGE

THE INK TANK
FAX MESSAGE

THE INK TANK
FAX MESSAGE

The Ink Tank
illustration agency
New York
USA

David Hockney
artist
Los Angeles
USA

to.

company.

from.

reference.

date.

no. of pages. this is page one.

if you do not receive all pages
please call the number below sharpish!

0742 754 982

デヴイナースリパフリック

99. design. ƐƳƆ.r3PU8l1c.

By appointment for the Future. 99.

the designers republic.

address. 1 sidney street

city. sheffield

post code. s1 4rg.

international dialing code. +44 742

u.k. dialing code. 0742

voice. 754 982.

u.k. dialing code. 0742

facsimile. 759 127.

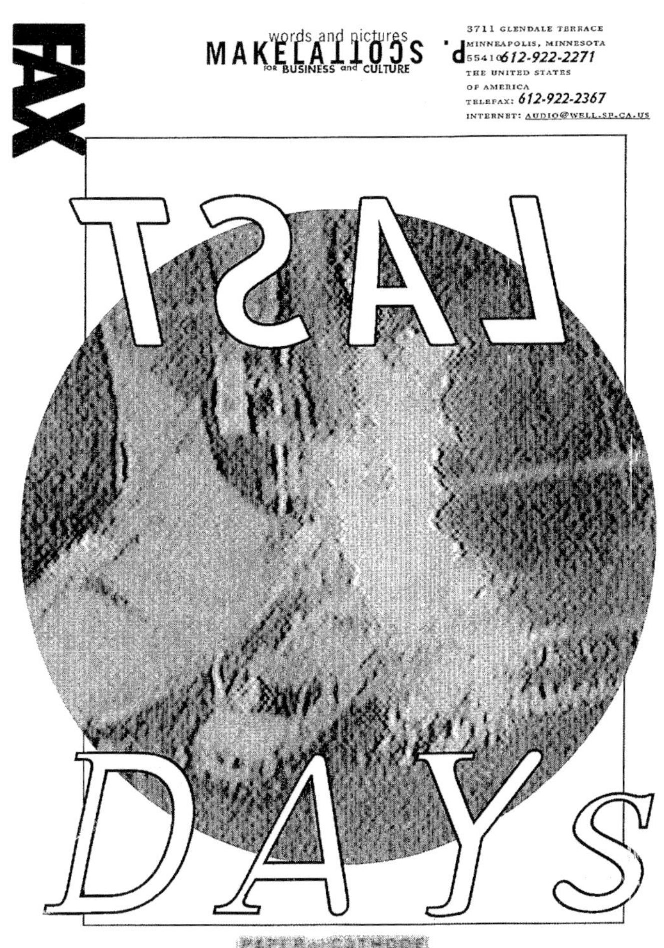

FAX
words and pictures
P. SCOTT MAKELA
FOR BUSINESS and CULTURE
3711 GLENDALE TERRACE
MINNEAPOLIS, MINNESOTA
55410 612-922-2271
THE UNITED STATES
OF AMERICA
TELEFAX: 612-922-2367
INTERNET: AUDIO@WELL.SF.CA.US
LAST
DAYS

The Designers
Republic
graphic designers
Sheffield
UK

P. Scott Makela
graphic designer
Minneapolis
USA

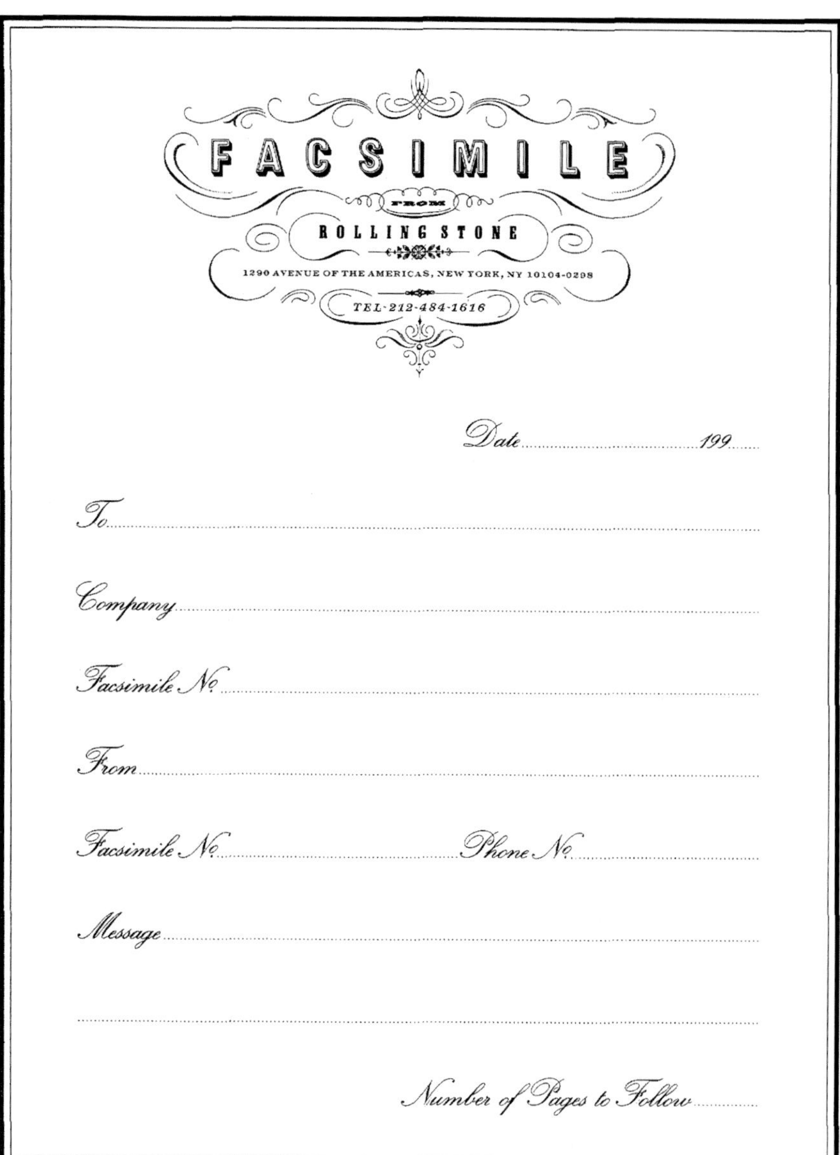
FACSIMILE
FROM
ROLLING STONE
1290 AVENUE OF THE AMERICAS, NEW YORK, NY 10104-0298
TEL-212-484-1616

Date .... 199.....

To ....

Company ....

Facsimile No. ....

From ....

Facsimile No. .... Phone No. ....

Message ....

....

Number of Pages to Follow ....

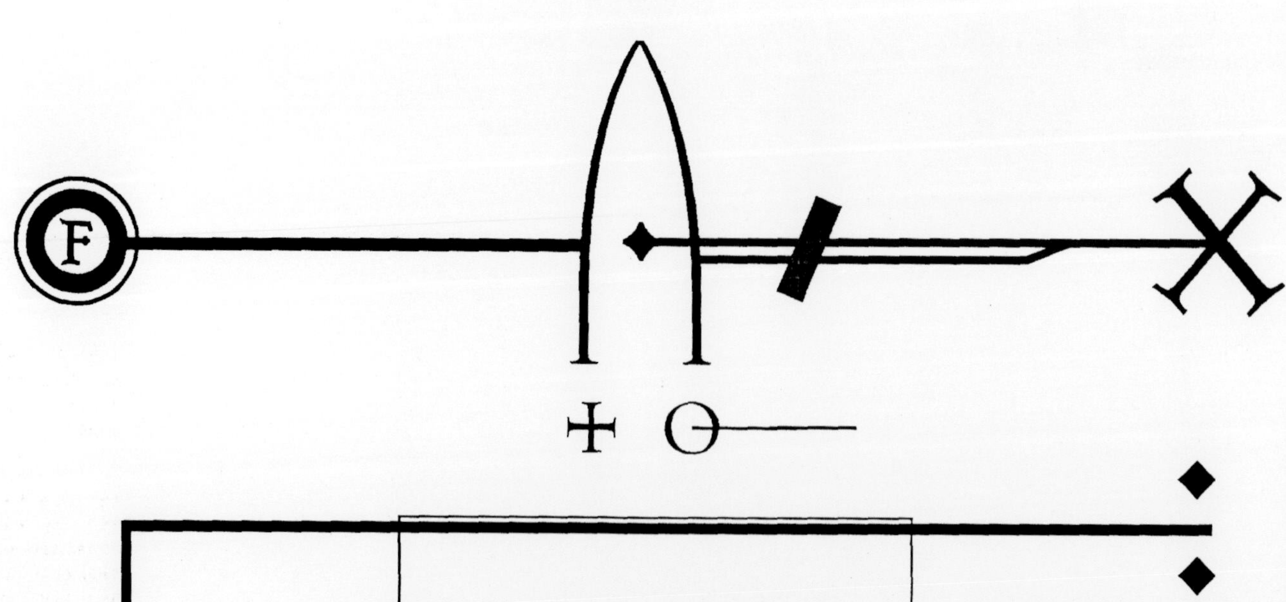

Fax

TO:

FROM:

FAX NUMBER:

PAGES *to* FOLLOW:

Rolling Stone
music magazine
New York
USA

Jonathan Barnbrook
graphic and typeface designer
London
UK

The Hoefler Type Foundry Inc
Jonathan Hoefler
typeface designer
New York
USA

MetaDesign West • Jeff Zwerner
300 Broadway Suite 29
San Francisco, CA 94115
Phone 415. 627. 0790
Fax 415. 627. 0795

MetaFax →

415. 627. 0790

Pages **Date**

San Francisco

West

Berli

TOUCH FAX

13 Osward Road London SW17 7SS

+ 44 (81) 682 3414

Editorial: (71) 704 2445

MetaDesign West
design consultancy
San Francisco and
Berlin
USA and Germany

Eye 2 Eye
graphic designers
Amsterdam
The Netherlands

<u>Touch</u>
audio-visual magazine
Jon Wozencroft
writer, designer,
publisher
London
UK

d a v i d CARSON design

1 2 8 . 5 th st
Del Mar CA 92014

pho 619 4 8 1
0 6 0 9
fax 481.4183

2:

VORM'GEVING ~S INSTITUUT

The Netherlands Design Institute

+31 20 6201003

Faxbericht

Stichting Het Nederlands Vormgevingsinst

Datum

Keizersgracht 560/562

Postbus 15797

1001 NG Amsterdam

T +31 20 638 11 20

Aantal bladen (inclusief voorblad)

1

Van

Aan

Tav

Faxnummer

Betreft

Aufuldish '& Warinner 183 the Alameda San Anselmo California 94960

FAXFROM { Bob Aufuldish 415 721.7921
Kathy Warinner 415 721.7920

date ....

pages ....

to ....

attn ....

re ....

notes

If this transmission is unclear,
please contact us at the above number

calling ....

Jean Marc Patras
69 rue de Turenne
75003 Paris
T: (331) 42 72 23 88
F: (331) 40 27 96 36

David Carson
magazine and graphic
designer
Del Mar
USA

Vorm'Geving Instituut
design institute
Amsterdam
The Netherlands

Aufuldish & Warinner
graphic designers
San Anselmo
USA

Jean Marc Patras
artist
Paris
France

Image
mnipr
resol

net/o

esent

ution

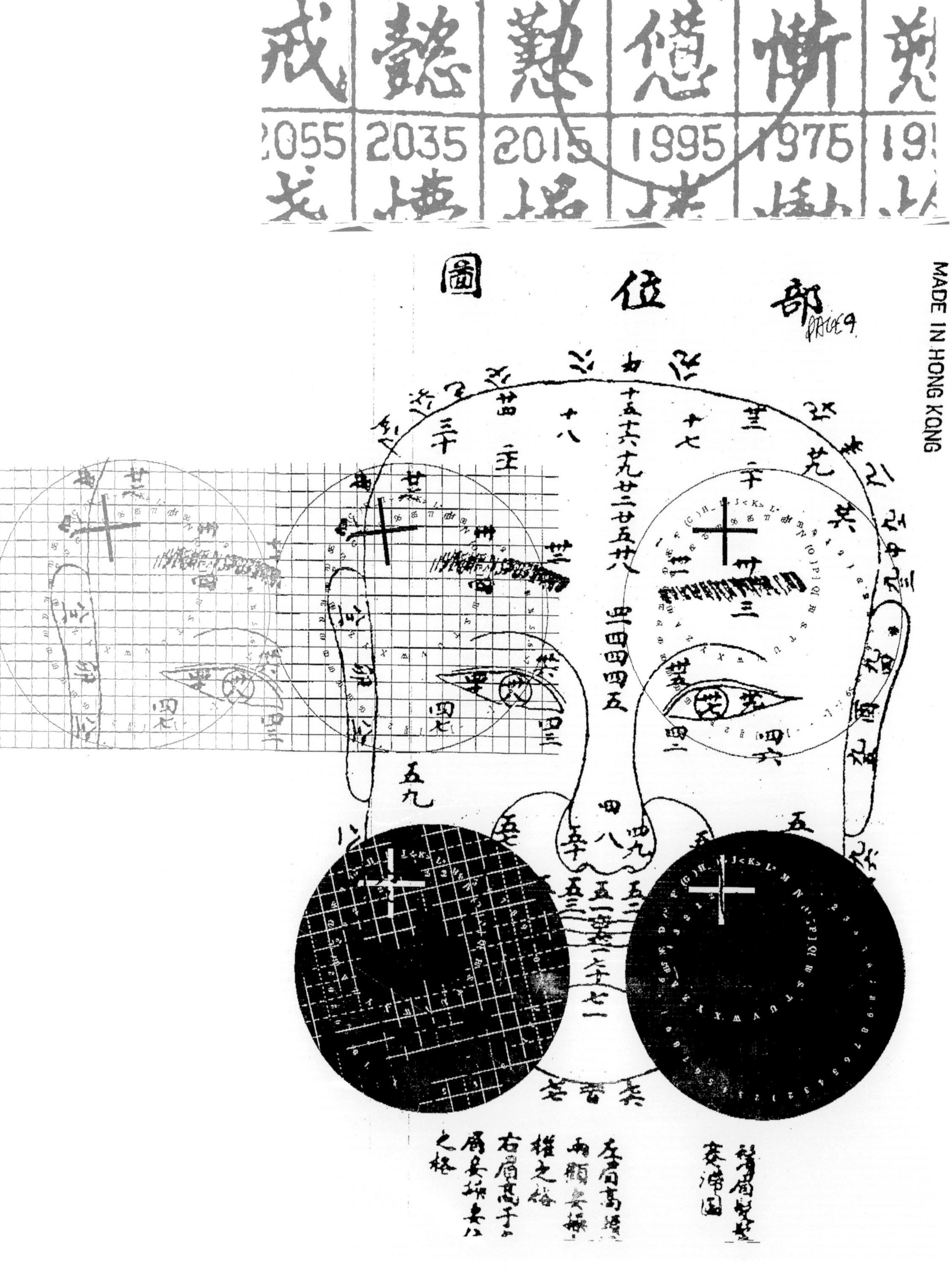
2055 2035 2015 1995 1975
部位圖
PAGE 9
MADE IN HONG KONG

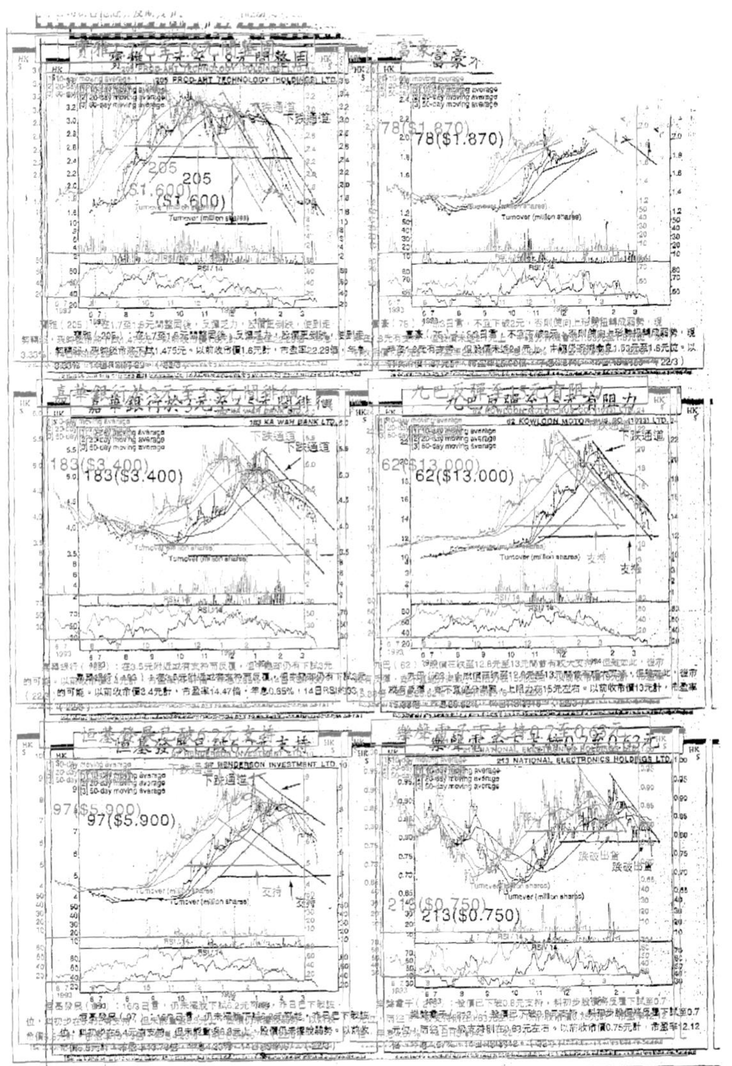

ID
David Bothwell

+852 815 6377

date
1994 03 24

duration
00 13' 02"

Hong Kong ephemera.

MOM'S CUTE
IN A LIVED
IN SORT OF
WAY WHEN
SHE PUTS ON
HER RED
SKIRT.
THE CURL IN
HER HAIR
ISN'T QUITE
WHAT IT
USED TO BE.

ID
Matt Eller
Walker Art Center

+1 612 375 7687

date
1994 04 18

duration
00 06' 02"

"An announcement sent to my friends and family introducing a typeface derived from my Dad's handwriting."

blue

ID
Simon Taylor

+44 71 434 0935

date
1992

by hand

Type for "Birth of the Cool" clothing label.

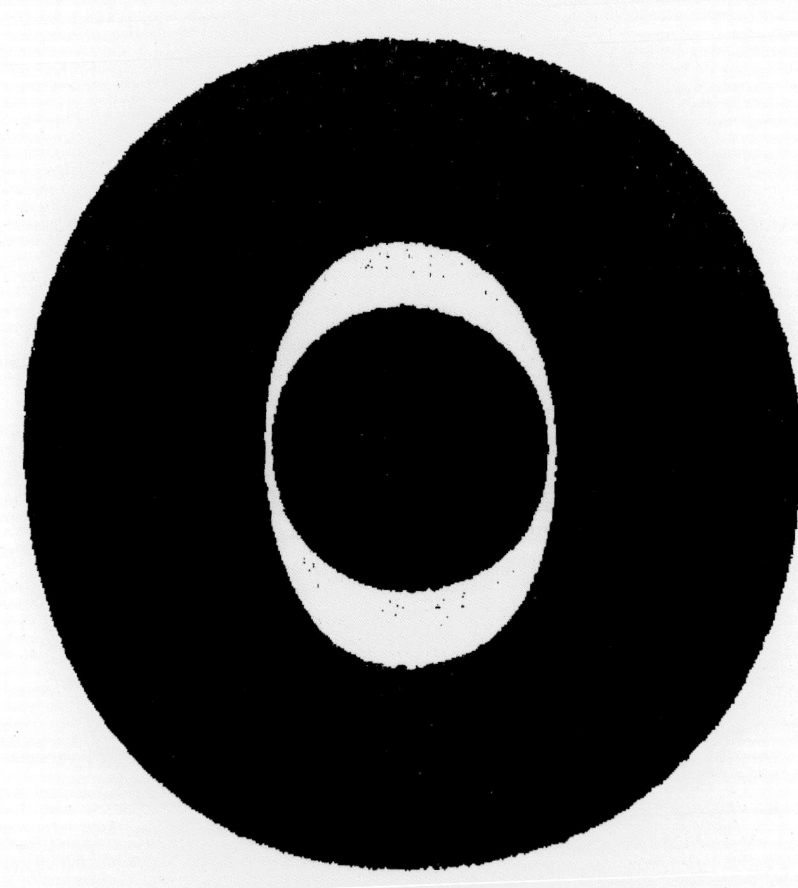

Trippy Helvetica (with dilated pupils)

blendo
dangerosi

say cheese

ID
Bob Aufuldish
Aufuldish & Warinner

+1 415 383 6139

date
1994 03 13

duration
00 03' 15"

"One of the joys of graphic design is the ephemeral nature of the work. Rather than a grand statement each piece is, instead, a siezed moment and is treated as such. What I like about faxes is that they are even more ephemeral. Even less precious. Part of the fun of faxes is there is absolutely no pressure to make something other than ordinary, allowing me to make things free of artifice. Unfortunately, all this will disappear once everyone is 'on line'. Documents - electronic and otherwise - will flow through the net; ephemeral things will never make it to paper. They will cease to exist."

Sardine Light

Sardine Light

Sardine Light

REWARD

ID
Tucker Viemeister to Rick Vermeulen
Smart Design to Hard Werken

+1 212 243 8514
+31 20 669 3144

date
1994 03 31

duration
00 04' 02"

"Here are a few special faxes. The 'Kat' series between me and Rick Vermeulen resulted in a design for the Sardine Light package!"

TIME
Job
Panic
Workers in the
world's richest
countries are in
a crisis,
in sight

TIME
The Great
American
JOB
End of an Era
Here is a subhed
r the interested
eader to get into
he good story that
is on
over this
EXIT

ID
Peter Kuper

+1 212 864 5729

date
1994 05 07

duration
00 21' 55"

The process of producing an illustration, communicating via fax, from rough to front cover for <u>Time</u> magazine.

ID
Gary Baseman

+1 718 499 9358

date
1994 04 27

duration
00 09' 02"

ID
Ian Warner
University of Portsmouth

+44 705 842077

date
1994 04 28

duration
00 01' 59"

ID
Jon Wozencroft

+44 71 704 2447

date
1994 05 13

duration
00 47' 56"

"Once Adobe Photoshop arrived I found myself using the fax machine less and less as a tool. But for a time it was central to much of the stuff I was doing. 'Dummy cover for the Spiral series, Touch 1989', I couldn't get my hands on a suitable spiral, so I created this shimmer effect on these cirlces by sending them back and forth through the fax.'Photocopy everything' was used as a tinted background for the pamphlet Xerox and Infinity, (Touchepas, 1991). For this effect I used a combination of photocopy, photoshop and fax. 'Frontispiece for Vagabond, 1991', the white areas were created by squirting Spray Mount on to thermal fax paper, waiting for it to dry and then reversing it out on the photocopier and re-faxing it."

1

2

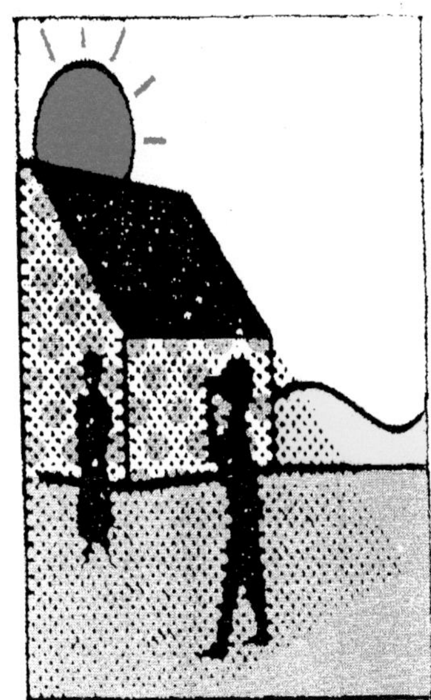

3

ID
Bless the Artist

+44 81 543 1398

date
1994 03 14

duration
00 03' 41"

Faxed colour
separations for
holiday postcards.

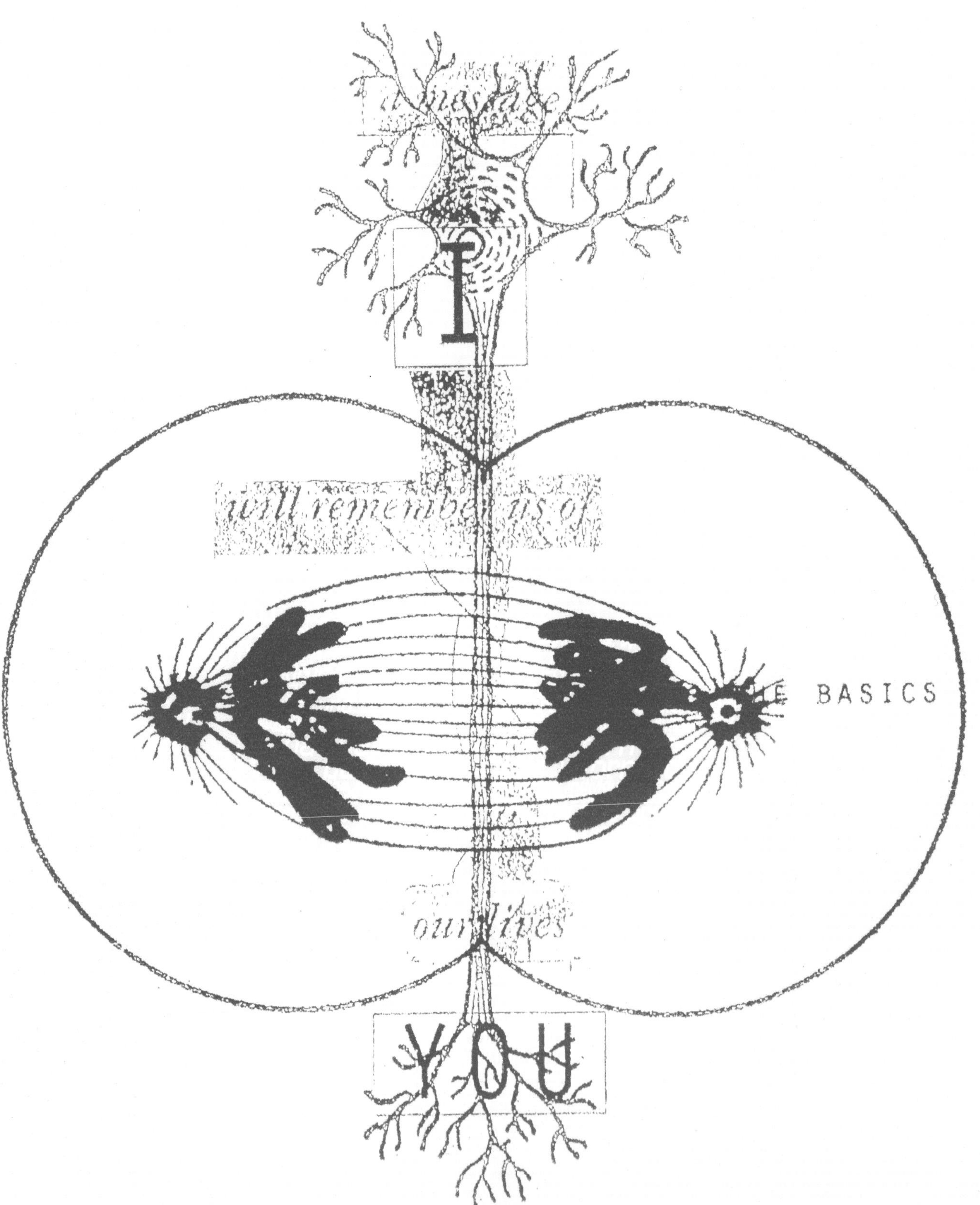

I
will remember us of
BASICS
our lives
YOU

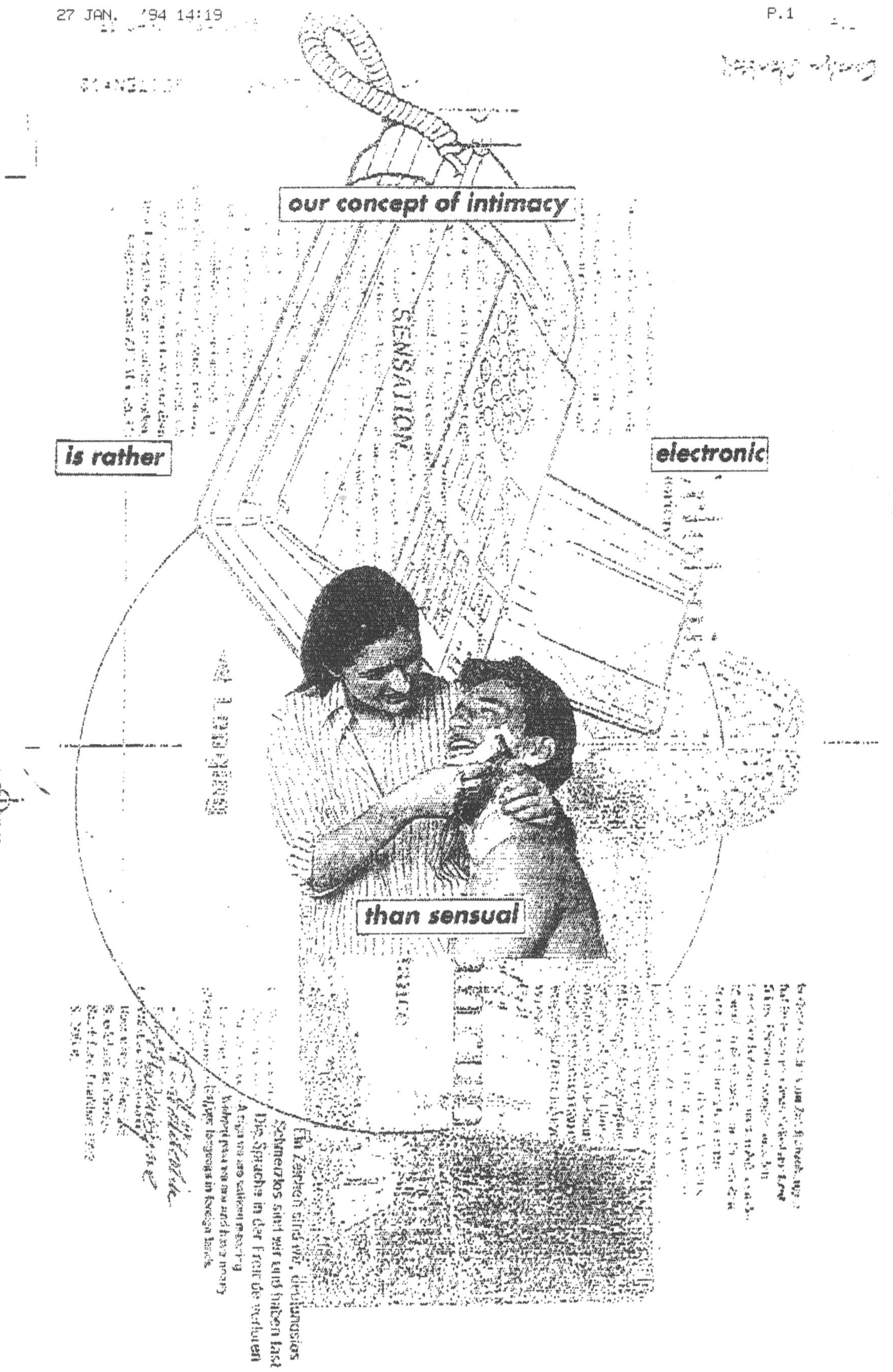

ID
Carolyn Steinbeck
and Thomas Noller

+1 810 645 3327
+49 69 496 0231

by post

"As graphic designers we are used to considering every element very carefully. Consequently we labour a long time over projects. Working with the fax machine, as a tool of communication, forces us to act more spontaneously. Sometimes I am very surprised about the resulting solutions. I see it as a good exercise to communicate messages effectively without concerning myself overly with stylistic elements. The fax machine has its own aesthetic which creates a new and different kind of quality. Thomas and I never really talk about the single pieces in our phone calls...there is no need for explanations. To me this fact represents one fundamental character of design work, namely its existence without accompanying verbal commentary. This work has to stand on its own. In our case the task of clear communication is less problematic because the audience is just one other person."

Facsimile

Betrifft / Reference / Objet

An / To / A

zu Hd. von / Attention / A l'Atte

Fax Nr.

0044-25 84 2077

Seitenzahl / Total Pages / Nb de

3

Zweckform Fax 1009

Date 28.1.94

Von / From / De

chspartner / Contact / Correspondent

Fax Nr. 340-6508226

No.

26/02 '94 12:55 +49 6404 63841 BUERO B BULLA →→→ ENVIRONMENTAL ST

26/02 '94 12:56 +49 6404 63841 BUERO B BULLA →→→ ENVIRONMENTAL ST

fax emis par : 31942195 IHI VECTOR

10/20/93 10:09 614 292 0217 IND DESIGN

Department of Industrial Design

T·H·E OHIO STATE UNIVERSITY

Facsimile Transmission

0532 701702 LICS

002

0532 701702 LICS

003

20/01 '93 11:49 +49221318822 KH Koeln U. Ring

001

FACHHOCHSCHULE KÖLN

8/01 '94 15:13 FAX 32 2 2999284

1994-01-05 15:38 FROM 3 4346669 CEECAN270310DG10 →→→ ENVIRONMENTAL ST

TO 00944705842077 001 P.01

Rijkshogeschool Maastricht

faculteit der kunsten

KOMMISSION DER EUROPÄISCHEN GEMEINSCHAFTEN

GENERALDIREKTION X

Audiovisuelle Medien, Information, Kommunikation, Kultur

Kultur, Kommunikation und Europa der Bürger

Kultur

748833

Page 3

22/02 '94 14:41 0532 701702

001

LEEDS INDUSTRI

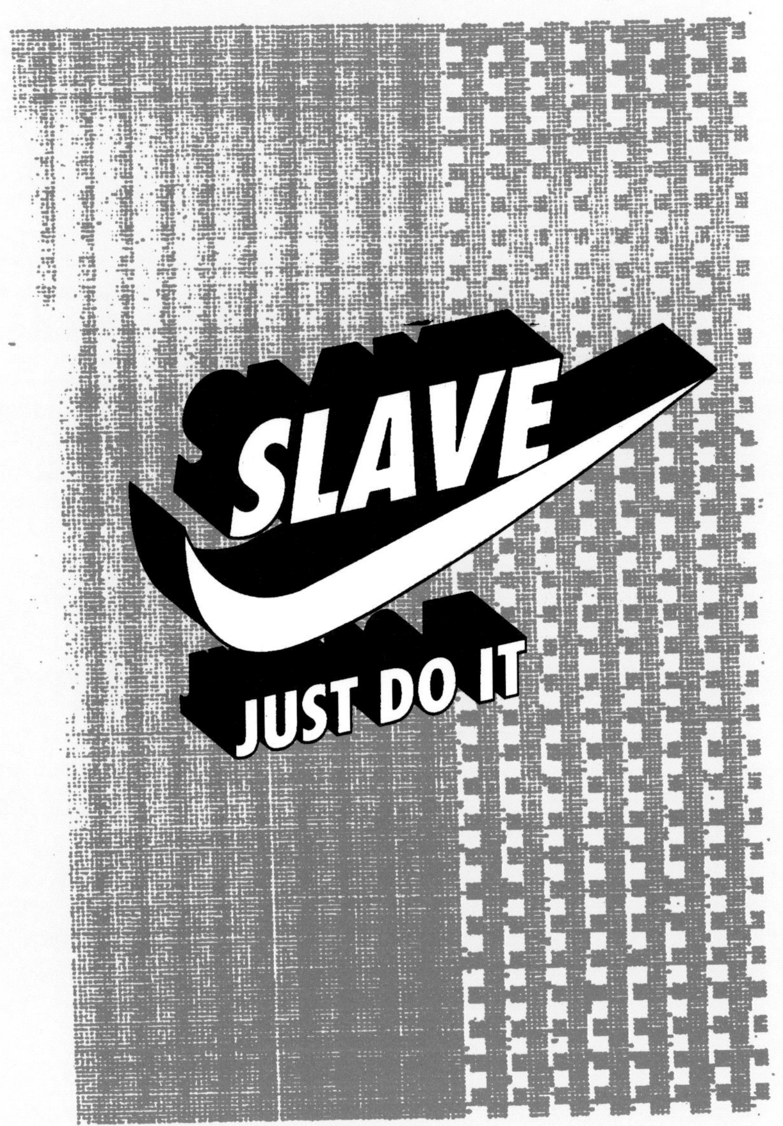

ID
Paul O'Connor
University of
Portsmouth

+44 705 842077

date
1994 04 28

duration
00 00' 45"

"Collage of incoming
fax message titles
(fax language)."

ID
The Corporate Slave

+44 51 709 9298

date
1994 04 21

duration
00 04' 56"

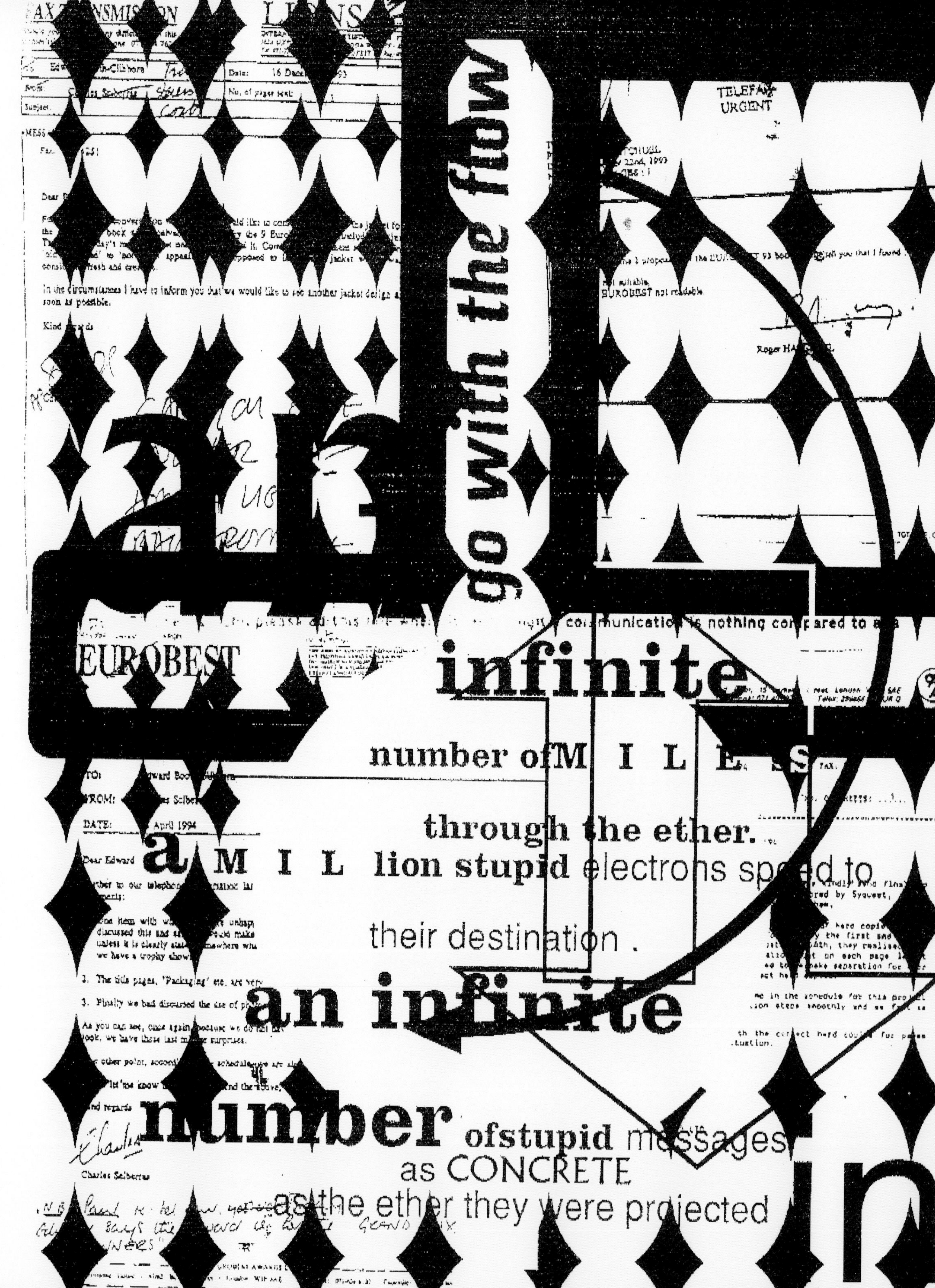
go with the flow
EUROBEST
communication is nothing compared to a
infinite
number ofM I L E S
through the ether.
a M I L lion stupid electrons speed to
their destination .
an infinite
number ofstupid messages
as CONCRETE
as the ether they were projected
TELEFAX
URGENT
Roger HA
In the circumstances I have to inform you that we would like to see another jacket design as
soon as possible.
Kind regards
TO:
FROM:
DATE:
Dear Edward
Charles Selberras

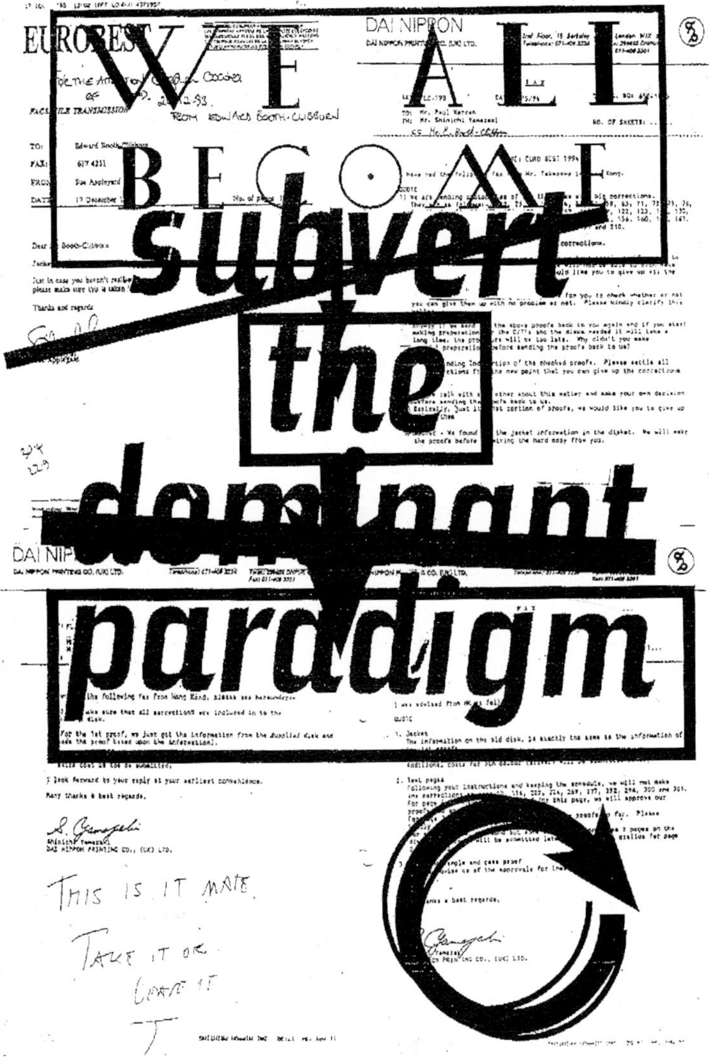

ID
Tony Arefin, Stephen Coates, Tony Arefin, Jonathan Barnbrook

+1 212 242 2066
+44 71 439 8561

date
1994 06 18

duration
00 04' 43"

From New York to London to New York to London, ex-studio colleagues contemplate the globalisation of graphic production.

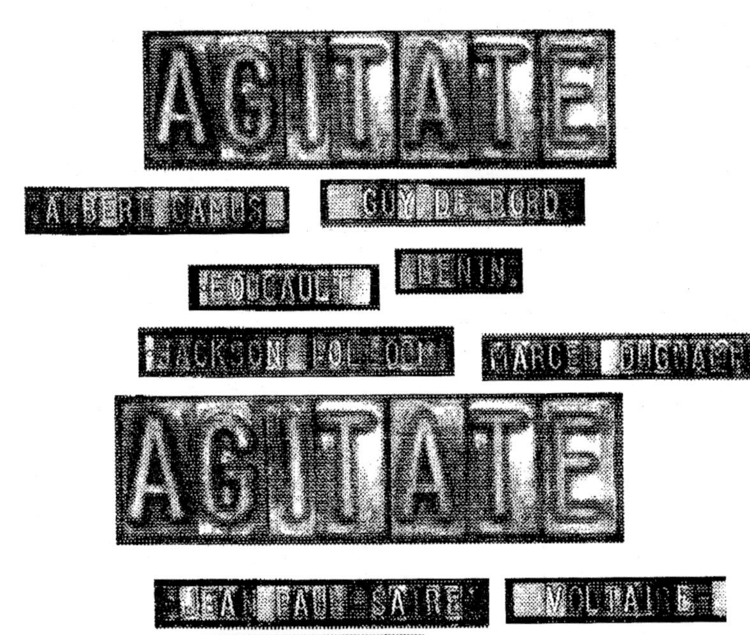

"URBAN * RE. ACTION

TUNE- UP,

TUNE- UP,

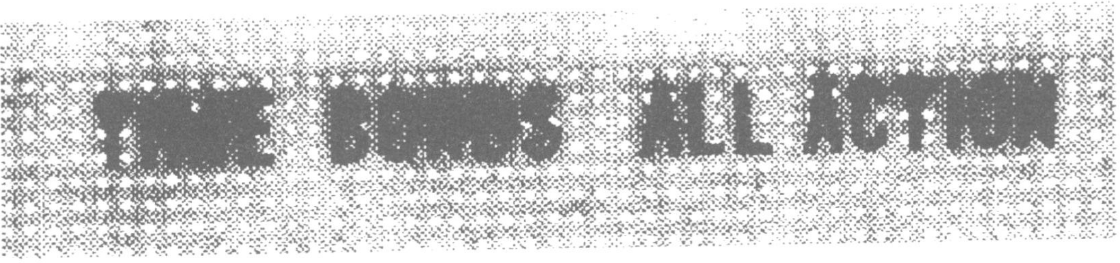

REVOLUTION,

EVOLUTION,

BOMB

ID
Simon Taylor

+44 71 434 0935

date
1994 06 20

duration
00 08' 13"

Designs for a clothing label sent by fax to Japan.

NOW THERE'S 34 B

FLYING

ROUND YOUR HEAD

YOU AIN'T DEAD F

NOW THERE'S 34 BIRDIES BIRDIES FLYI

BIRDIES

YOU

DING DING ROUND TWO

34'S BUTT COMES WITH

SCORE

ID
Graham Wood

+44 71 434 0935

date
1993

by hand

Type faxed to the client for approval which became a tv ad for Nike featuring the basketball player Charles Barkley.

ES

LUCKY

OUND YOUR HEAD

DING DING ROUND TW

OU AIN'T DEAD FRED LUCKY YOU

ID
Joanne Hassall

+44 81 543 1398

date
1993

by hand

Illustrations produced using a fax machine. Images were passed through the fax, photocopied onto acetate and layered over painted surfaces, different coloured papers and other printed material.

blue bottles
cigarettes
blood
light bulbs
ourescent lights
fishes

hairdressers

greasy ducks
toilet
tinwork
blood soaked cardboard

tins of sweetened milk

blue bottles
cigarettes
blood
light bulbs

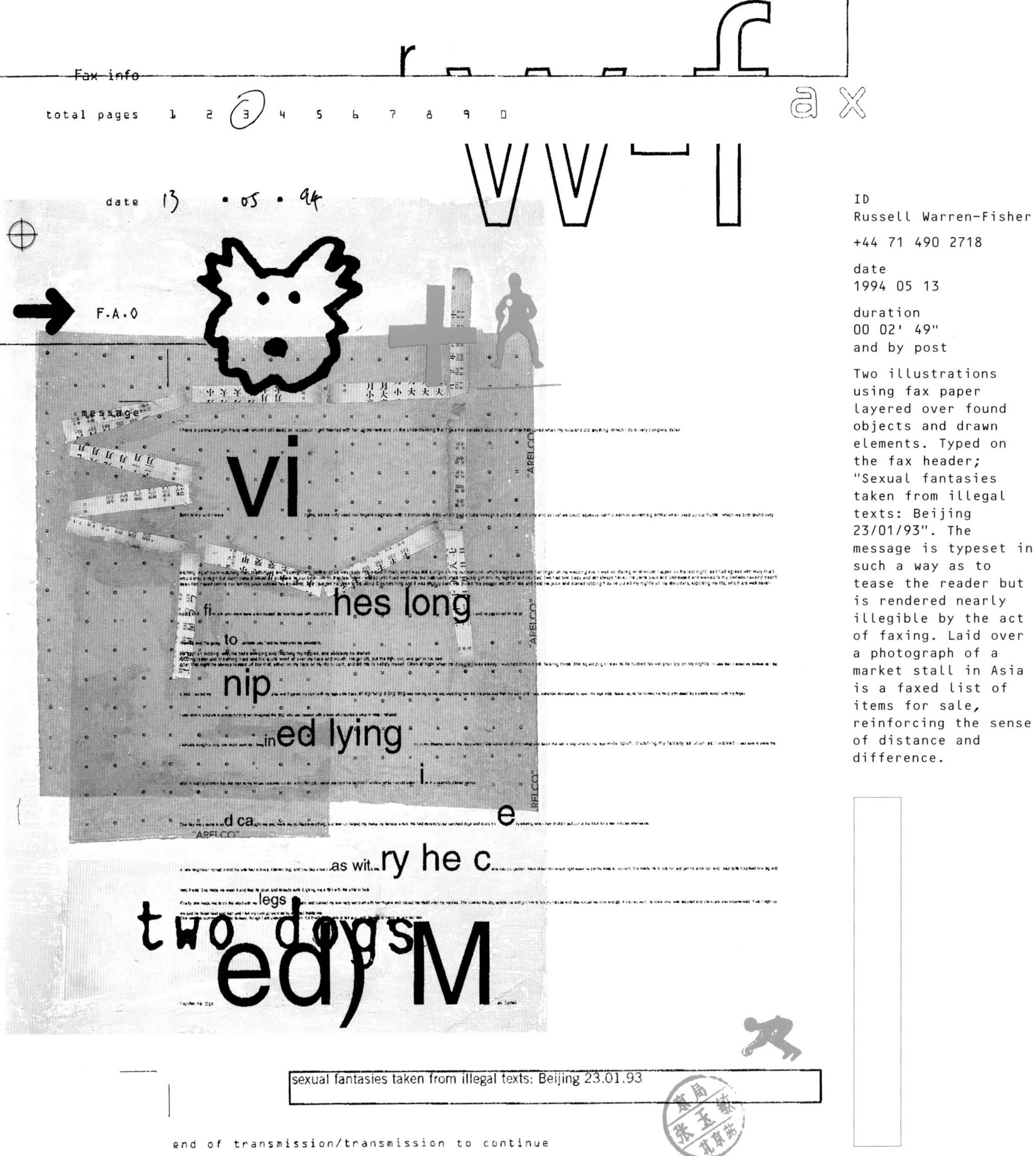

ID
Russell Warren-Fisher

+44 71 490 2718

date
1994 05 13

duration
00 02' 49"
and by post

Two illustrations using fax paper layered over found objects and drawn elements. Typed on the fax header; "Sexual fantasies taken from illegal texts: Beijing 23/01/93". The message is typeset in such a way as to tease the reader but is rendered nearly illegible by the act of faxing. Laid over a photograph of a market stall in Asia is a faxed list of items for sale, reinforcing the sense of distance and difference.

ABSOLUT FAX.

THERE IS NO PURER VODKA THAN ABSOLUT. DO IT JUSTICE. DRINK IT NEAT AT 0°C.

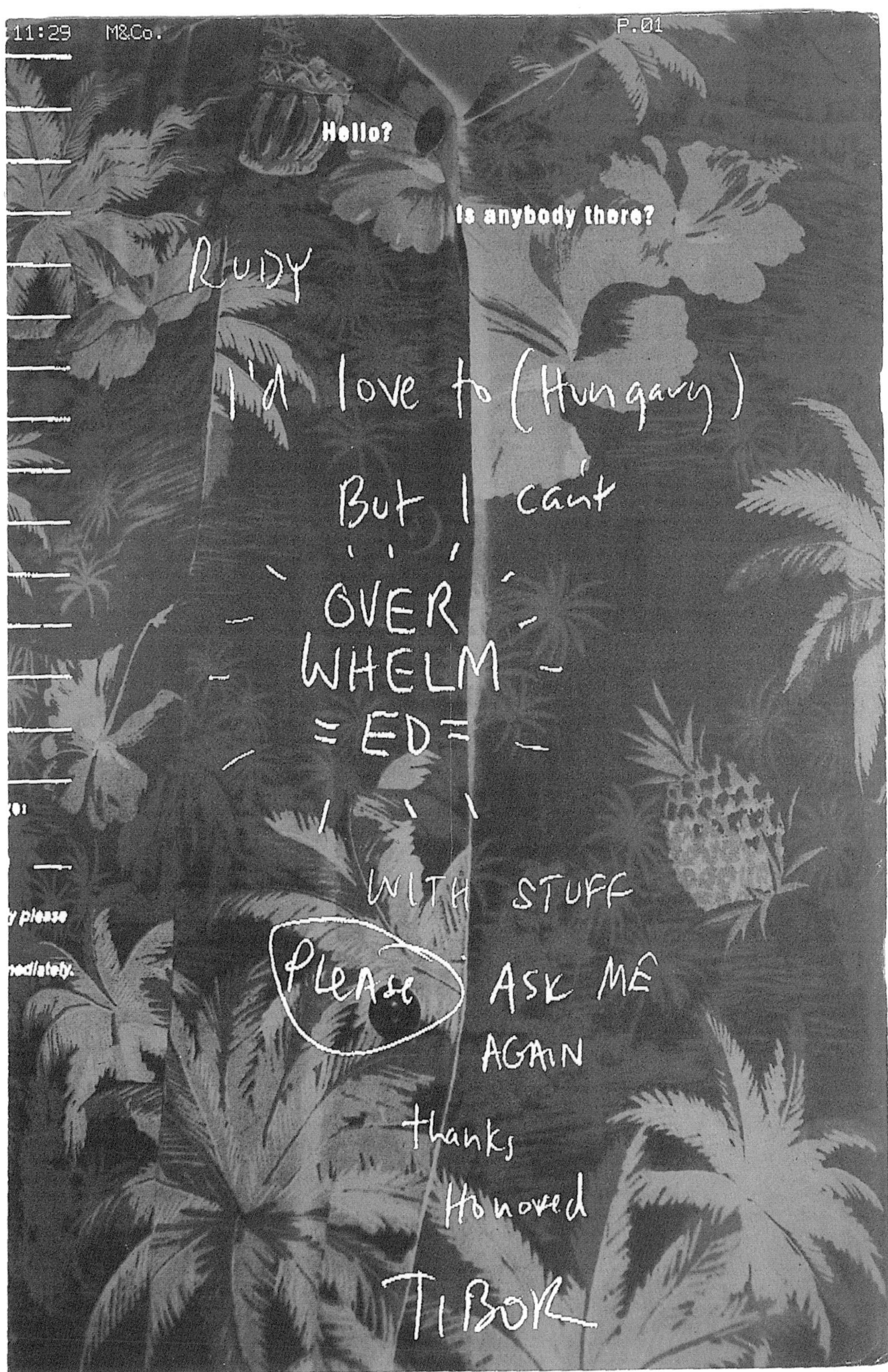

ID
Absolut Vodka

date
1994

Ad for the brand which promotes itself as an artwork. This "fax art" appropriation graces the pages of newspapers and the back covers of magazines.

ID
Tibor Kalman to Rudy VanderLans

+1 415 644 0820

date
<u>Emigre</u> #13 1989

A personally-penned apology.

Techn
notec

otech
hno

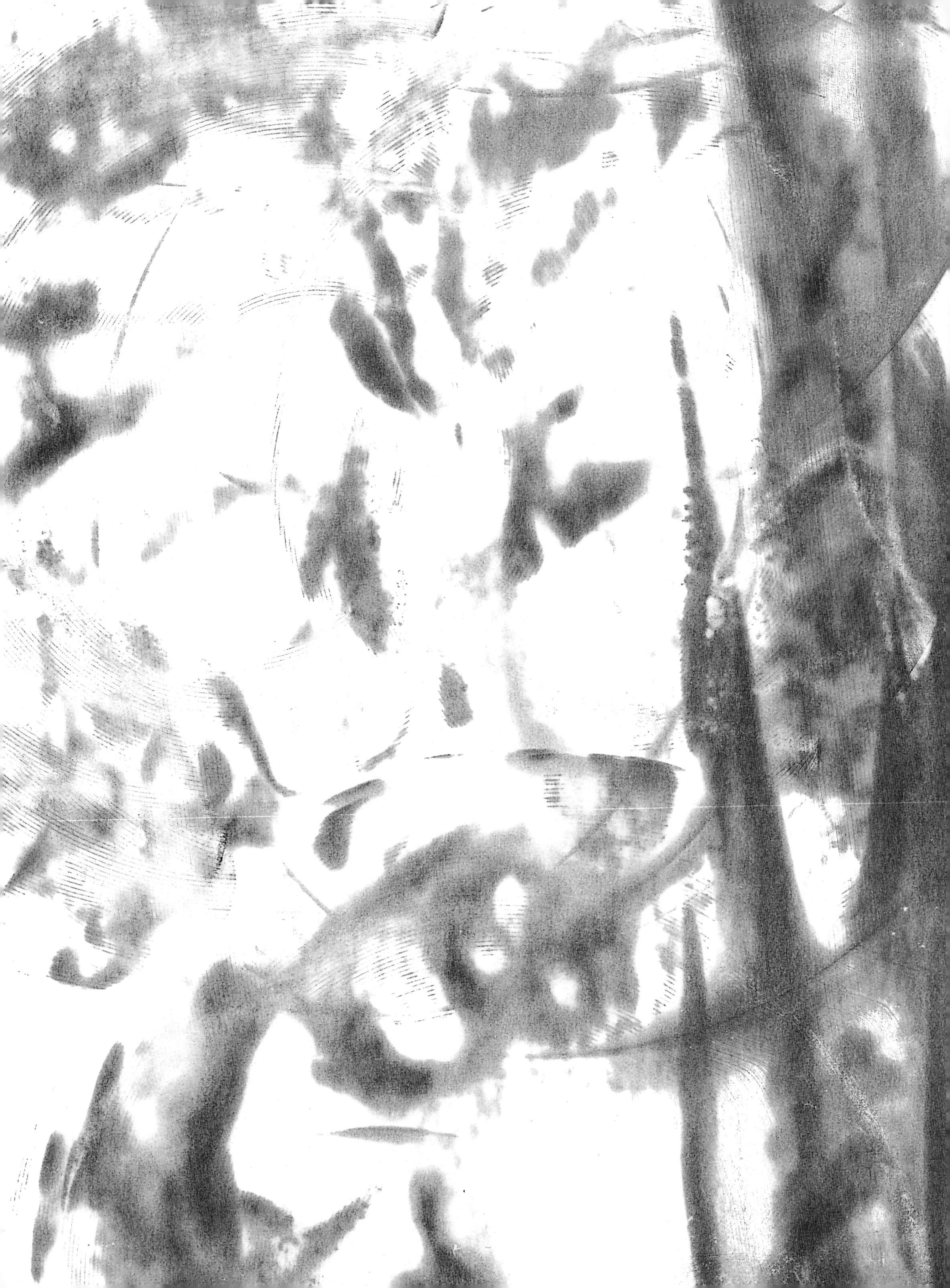

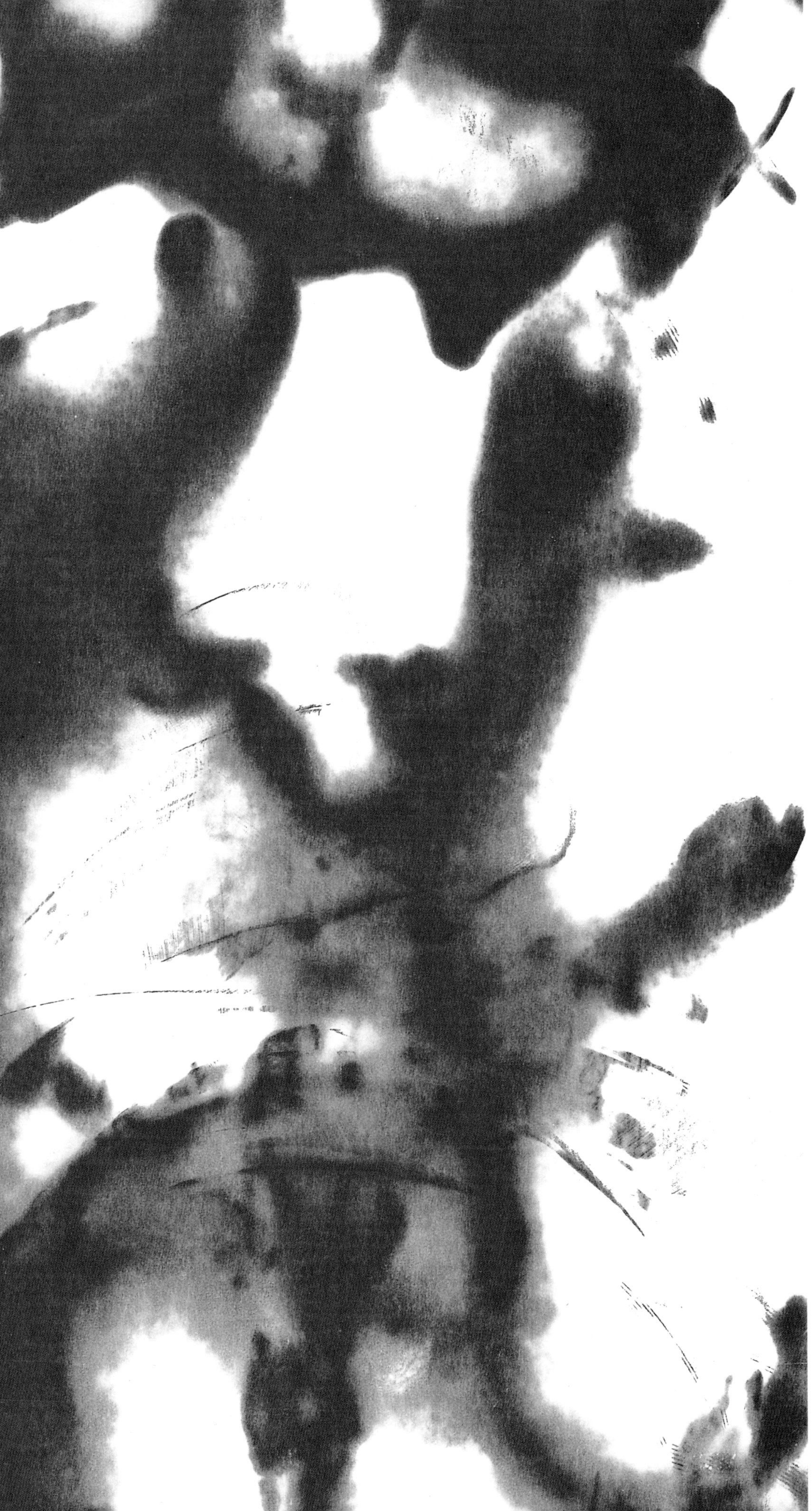

ID
John Warwicker and
Graham Wood

+44 71 434 0935

date
1993

by hand

"This is an 'energy fax'. In the spring of 1993 Graham and I were given a workshop at the Rodeckerhaus in Frankfurt and looking for something to illustrate our thoughts on process. We had brought several rolls of fax paper with us. We had the idea of using matches to make marks on the paper but soon realised the limitations...then we moved to the electric cooker. What excited us was the ability to draw with pure energy. The resulting piece was a roll long (100 metres) which we placed on a hillside and videoed. An extension of this idea is to have it traversing national borders as infomation ley lines. We have continued to produce these. This example is 50 metres long."

a a a a a a a a a a a a a a a a

b b b b b b b b b b b b b b b b b b b

c c c c c c c c c c c c c c c c c c

d d d d d d d d d d d d d d d d d d d d d

e e e e e e e e e e e e e e e e e e e e

f f f f f f f f f f f f

l l l l l l l

g g g g g g g g g g g g g g g

h h h h h h h h h h h h h h h h h h h h h h h

i i i i i i i i i i

j j j j j j j

k k k k k k k k k k k k k k k k k k k k k k k k k k

m m m m m m m m m m m m m m m m m m m m m m m

n n n n n n n n n n n n n n n n n

o o o o o o o o o o o o o o o o o o o o o o o o

p p p p p p p p p p p

p p p p p p p p p p p p

q q q q q q q q q q q q q q q q q q q q q q q q q q q

r r r r r r r r r r r r r r

s s s s s s s s s s s s s s s s s

t t t t t t t t t t t t t t t t

u u u u u u u u u u u u u u u u u u u u u u u u u u u

qwertyuiop
asdfghjkl
zxcvbnm

burnie inn

ID
Alex Pereira

+44 71 225 1487

date
1993–1994

by post

Experiments with heated metal type on thermal paper. The type imprints were scanned into a computer and converted into the typeface "Burnie Inn".

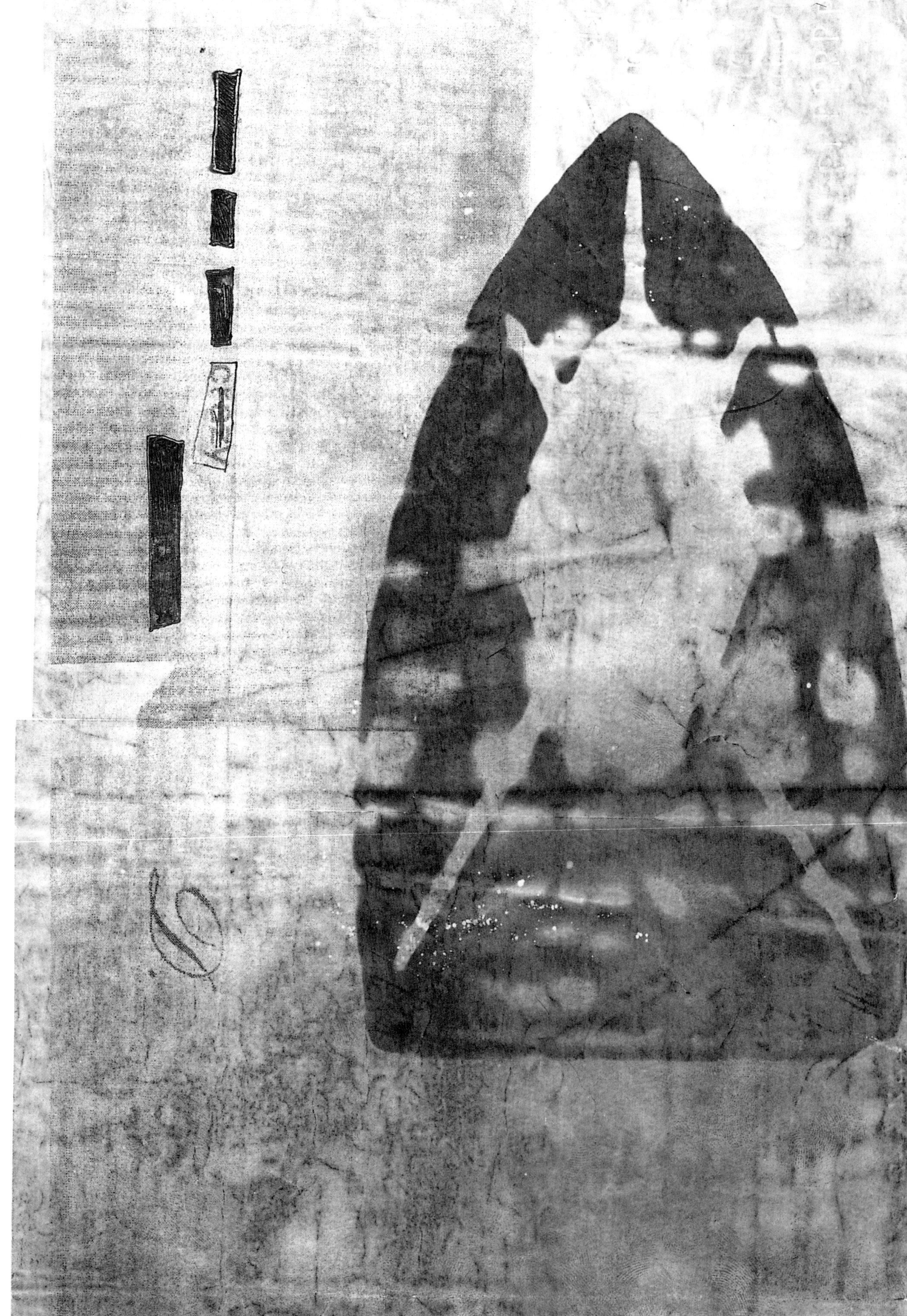

ID
Alex Pereira

+44 71 225 1487

date
1994

by post

Using a household iron on thermal paper and heat-sensitive till roll Pereira makes marks without ink.

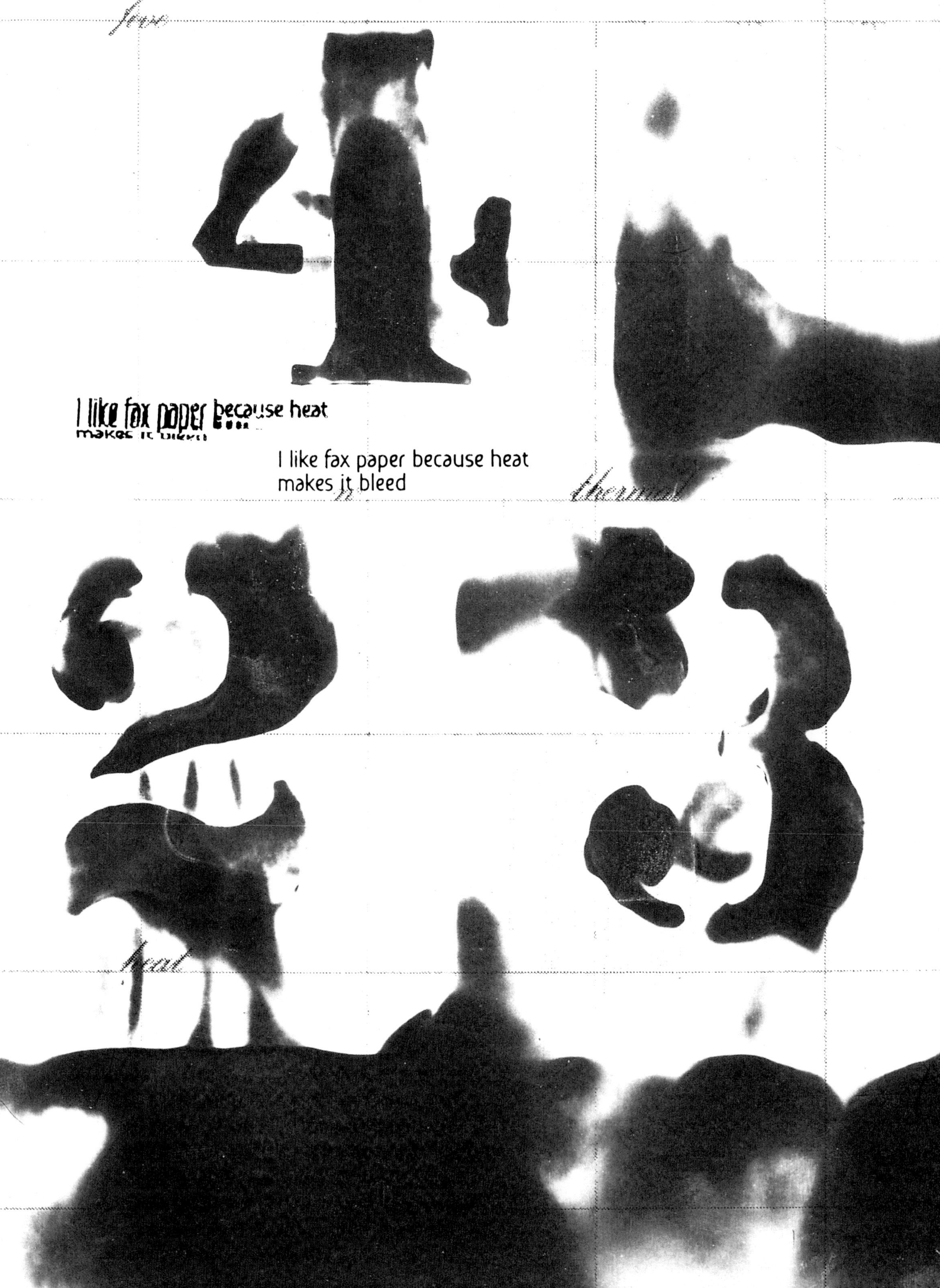
four
I like fax paper because heat
I like fax paper because heat
makes it bleed
thermal
heat

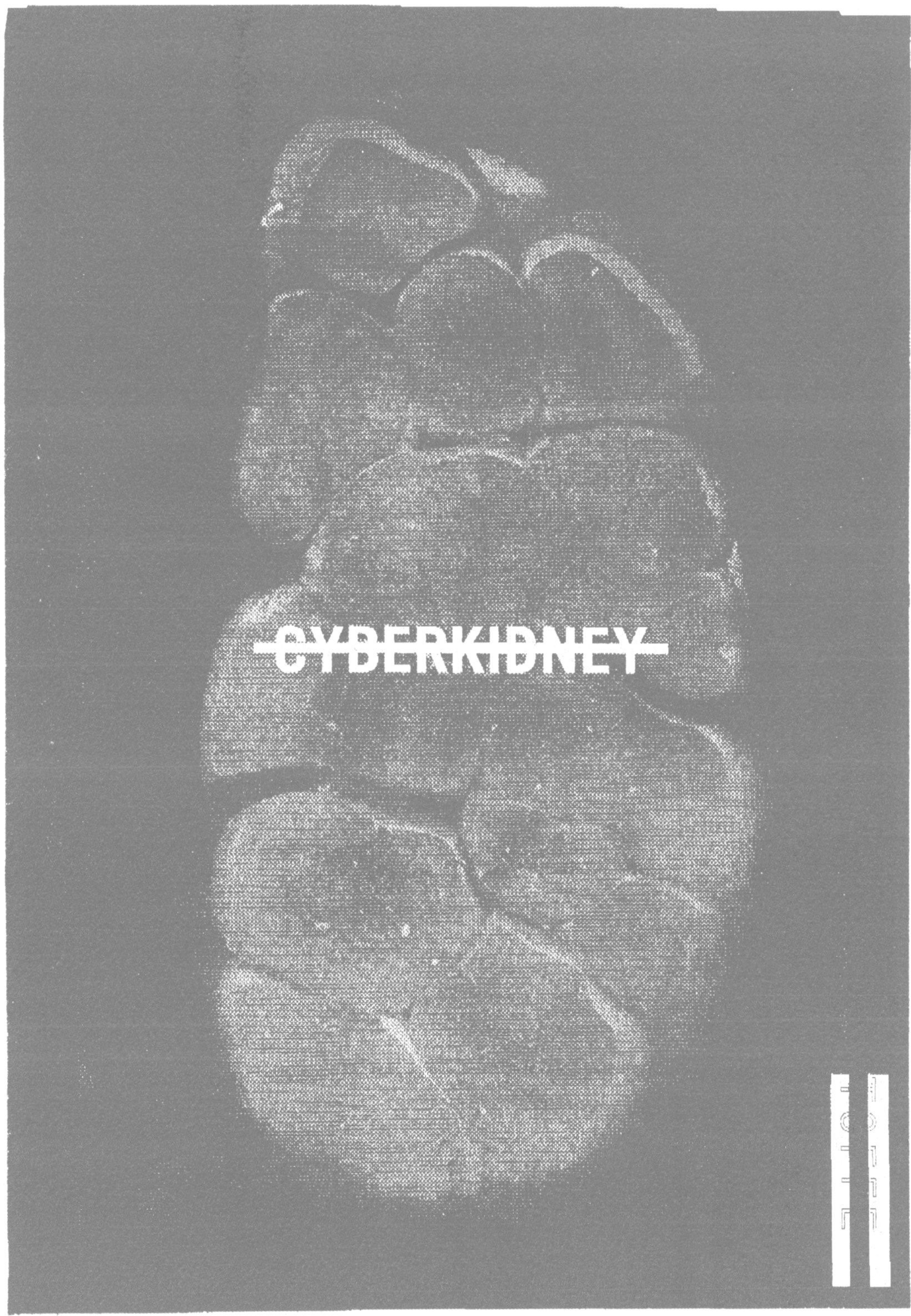

ID
Simon Manchipp

+44 71 221 2225

date
1994

by post

Observations on the nature of faxes. Written on the reverse of this image "Warning: Do not leave in direct sunlight".

ID
Toffe

+33 1 46 07 46 53

date
1994 05 28

duration
00 01' 56"

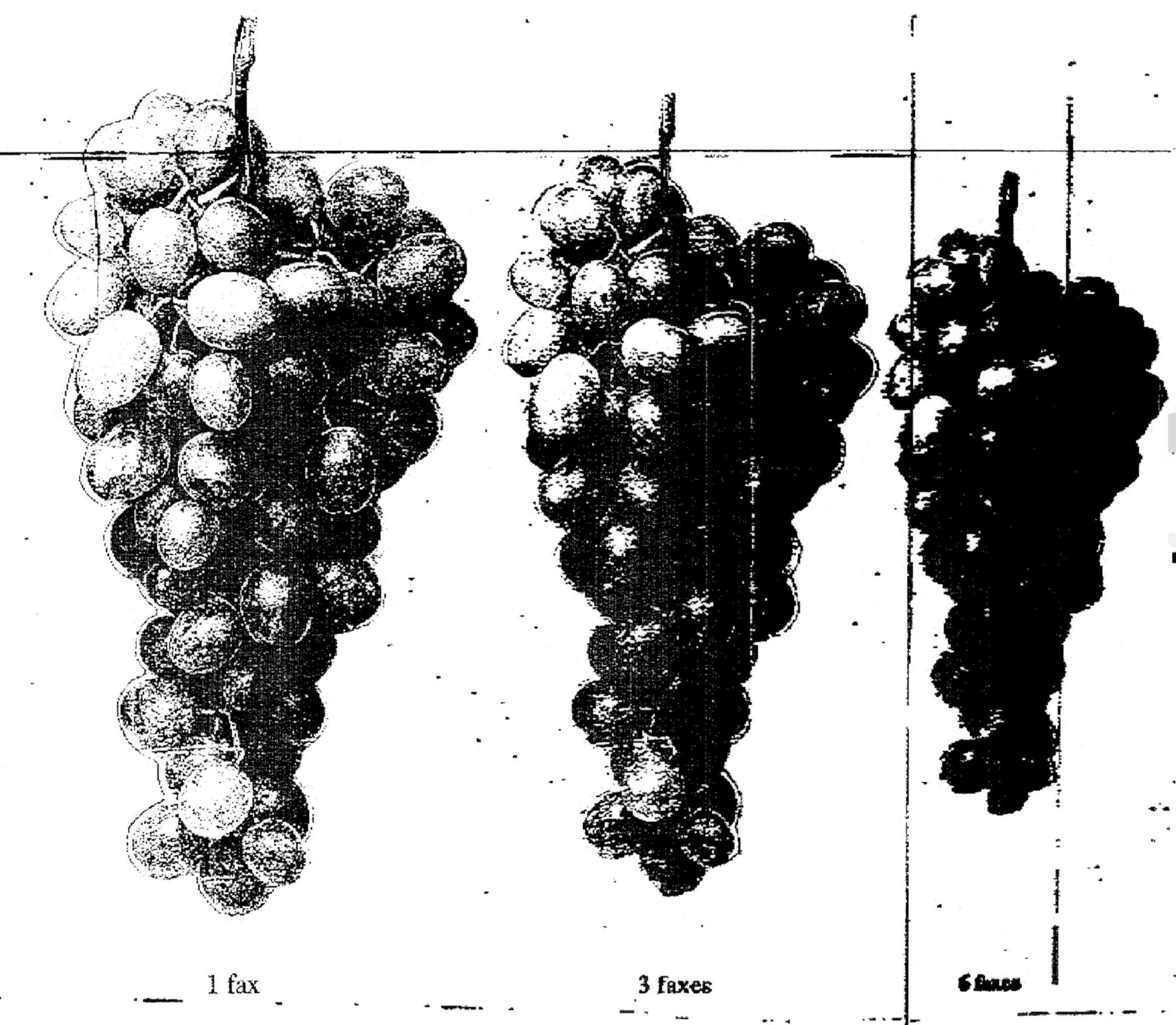
1 fax
3 faxes
6 faxes

ID
Michael Callan

+44 71 225 1487

date
1994 03 24

duration
00 01' 58"

The Decaying Image. "My aim was to show that the fax automatically diminishes and degenerates transmitted information. I used fruit to emphasise the decaying process."

ID
Why Not Associates

+44 71 494 0678

date
1994 04 20

duration
00 01' 34"

In memory of the British comedian, Les Dawson, recently deceased.

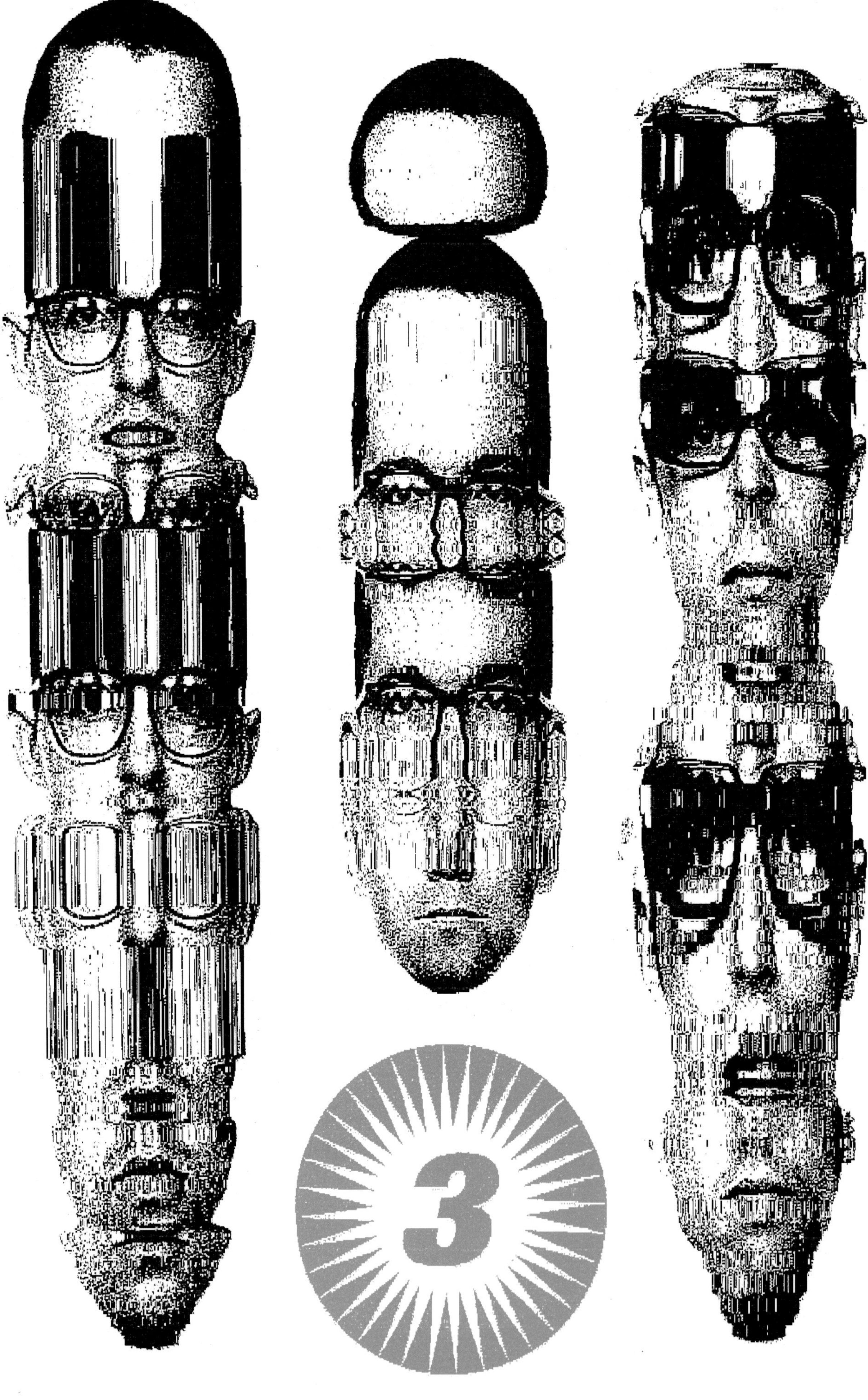
3

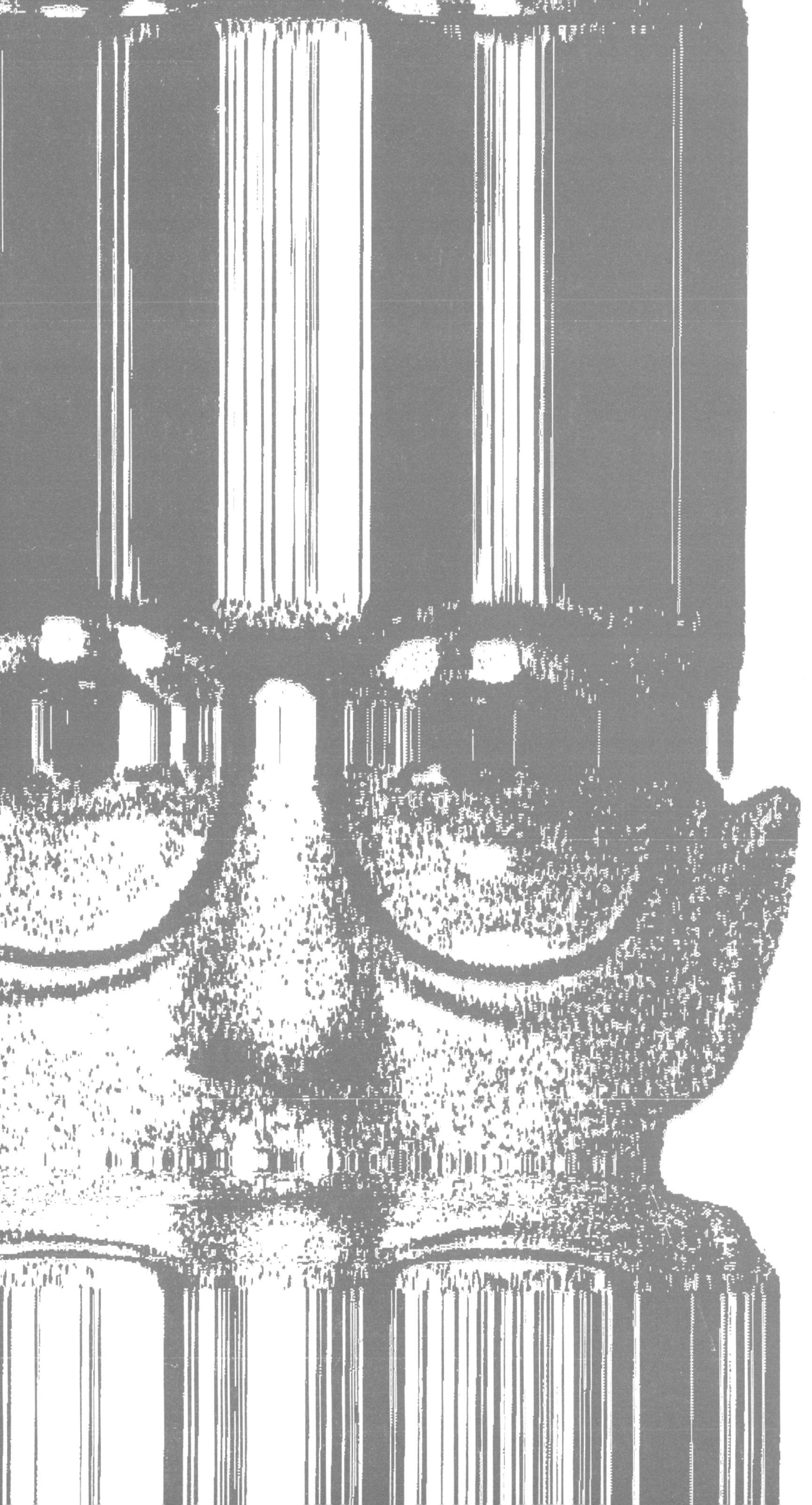

ID
Nice

+44 71 813 6179

date
1994 03 21

duration
00 08' 14"

During transmission this photograph was stalled to create a stretched and distorted group portrait of the designers, hinting at the commercial nature of graphic design through the accidental creation of bar-codes.

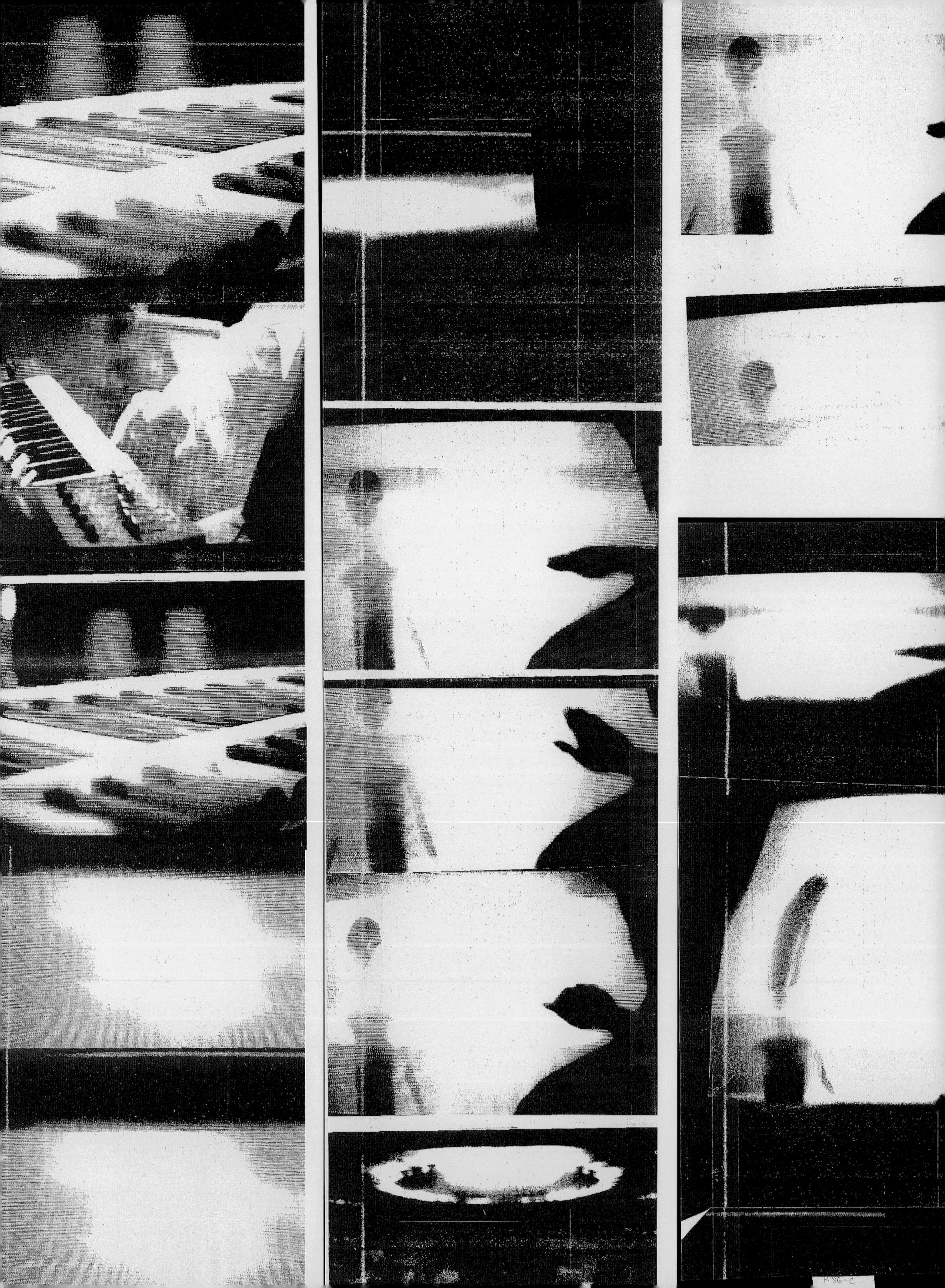

ID
Clive
Middlesex University

+44 81 362 5057

date
1994 05 12

duration
00 22' 05"

Faxed extracts from
a videoed "rave".

n de Republiek, 31 december 1989.

ID
gebr de Jong

+31 20 620 8368

date
1994 02 21

duration
00 10' 45"

FREE
LIFT RING
PUSH BACK
REGISTERED TRADE

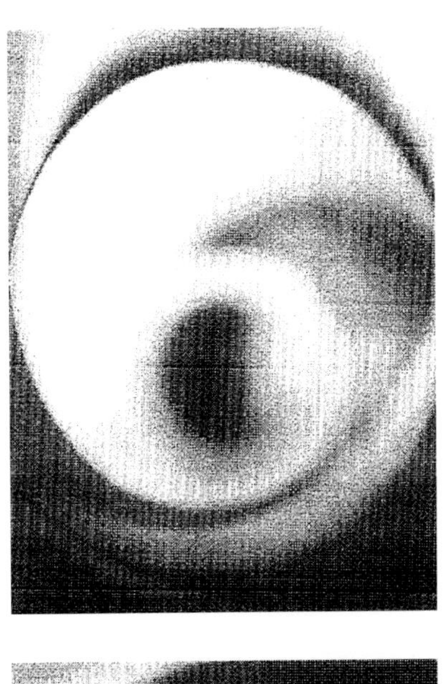

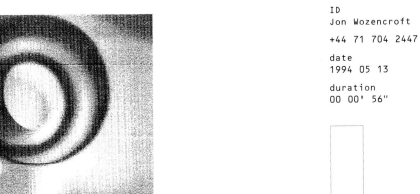

ID
Jon Wozencroft

+44 71 704 2447

date
1994 05 13

duration
00 00' 56"

ID
Arran Elvidge

+44 71 354 0098

date
1994

duration
00 00' 38"

Faxed photographs of thermal fax paper.

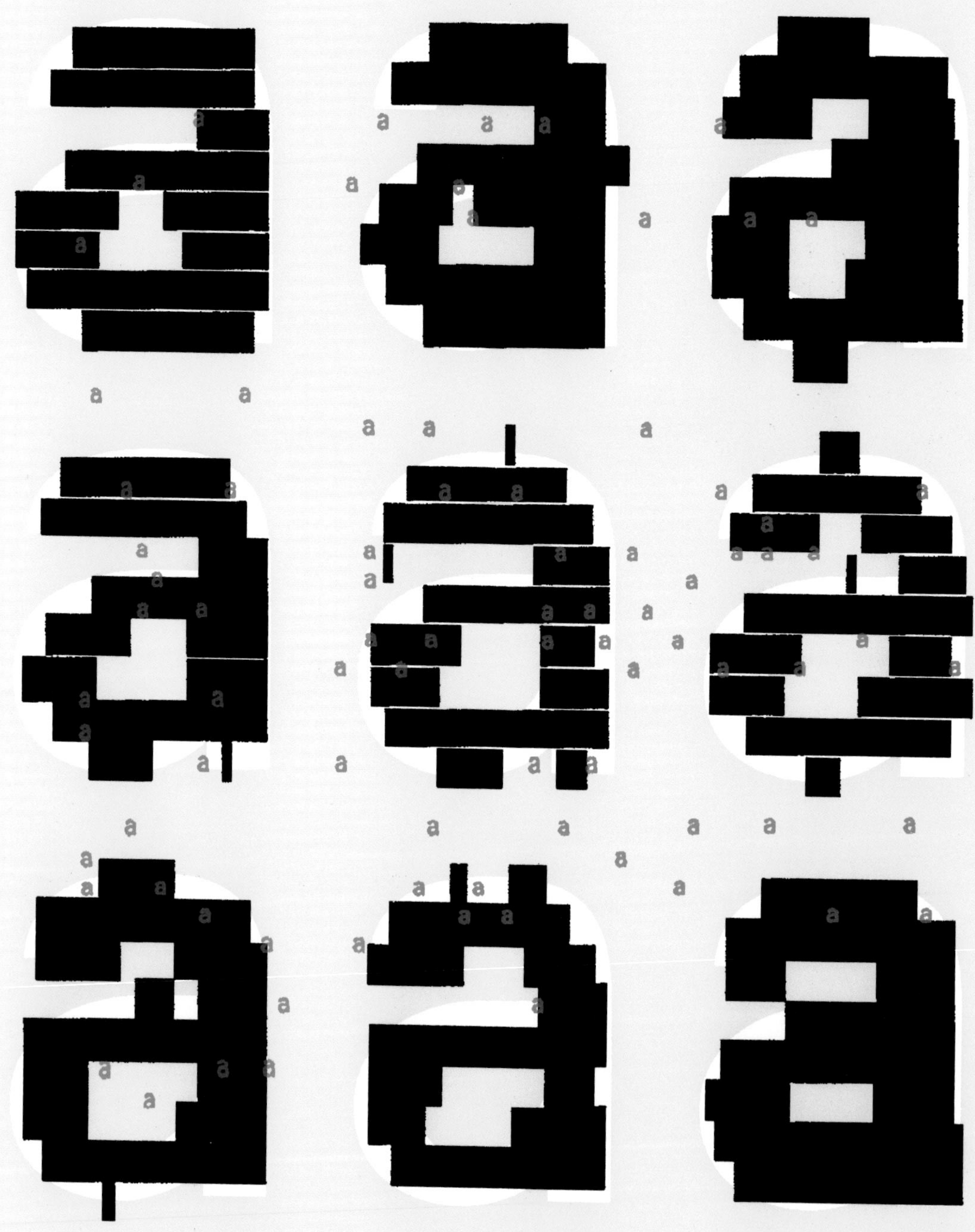

CADMIUM YELLOW

ID
Clifford Hiscock

+44 71 734 5097

date
1994 05 11

duration
00 02' 34"

"Both faxes are about the inaccuracy of fax communication. Firstly, what happens when the image is broken up into all those horizontal lines. The effect on type is an infinite number of interpretations of the same character. To illustrate this I selected 9 lower case OCR-B "a"s from the Urgent Images reminder fax, enlarged them, cleaned them up a bit and put them over the original letter forms. The second fax shows how different colours get reduced to either solid black or white."

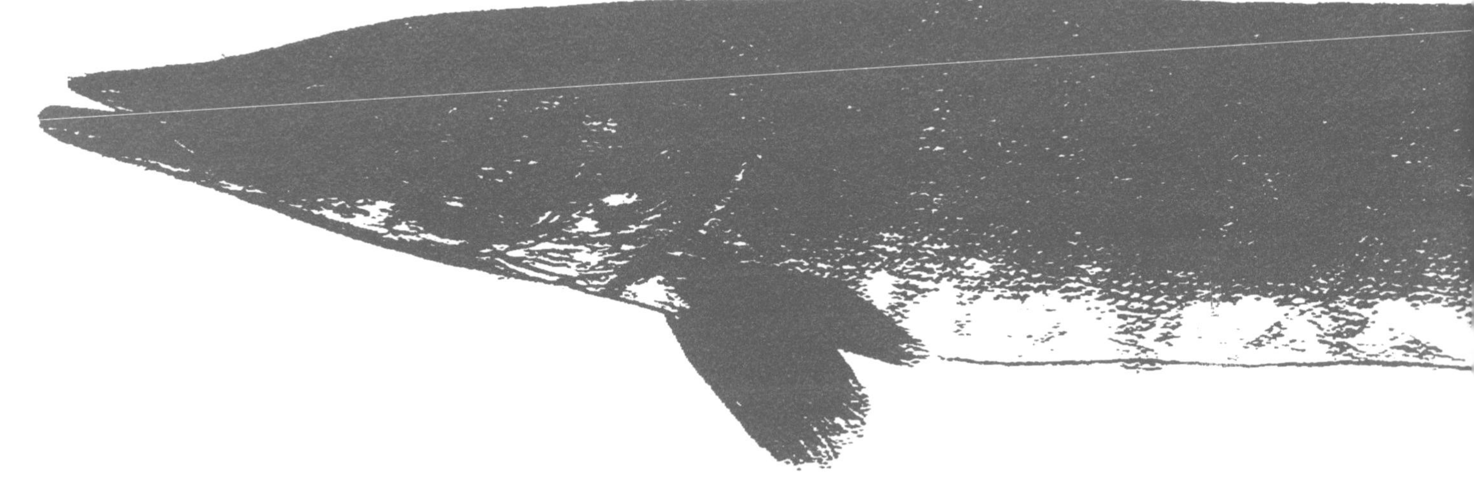

Bon appétite

ID
Kari Piippo

+358 55 162687

date
1994 05 13

duration
00 02' 46"

The continuous roll of fax paper can accommodate a fish which is larger than the standard A4 format.

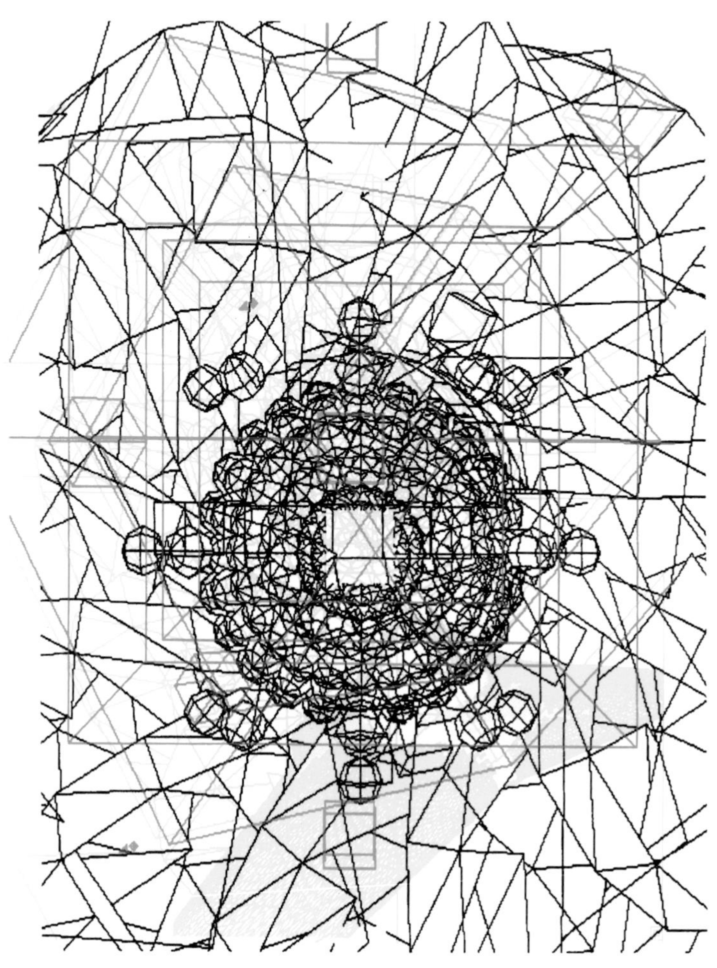

ID
The Corporate Slave

+44 51 709 9298

date
1994 04 21

duration
03 57' 01"

Faxed separations.

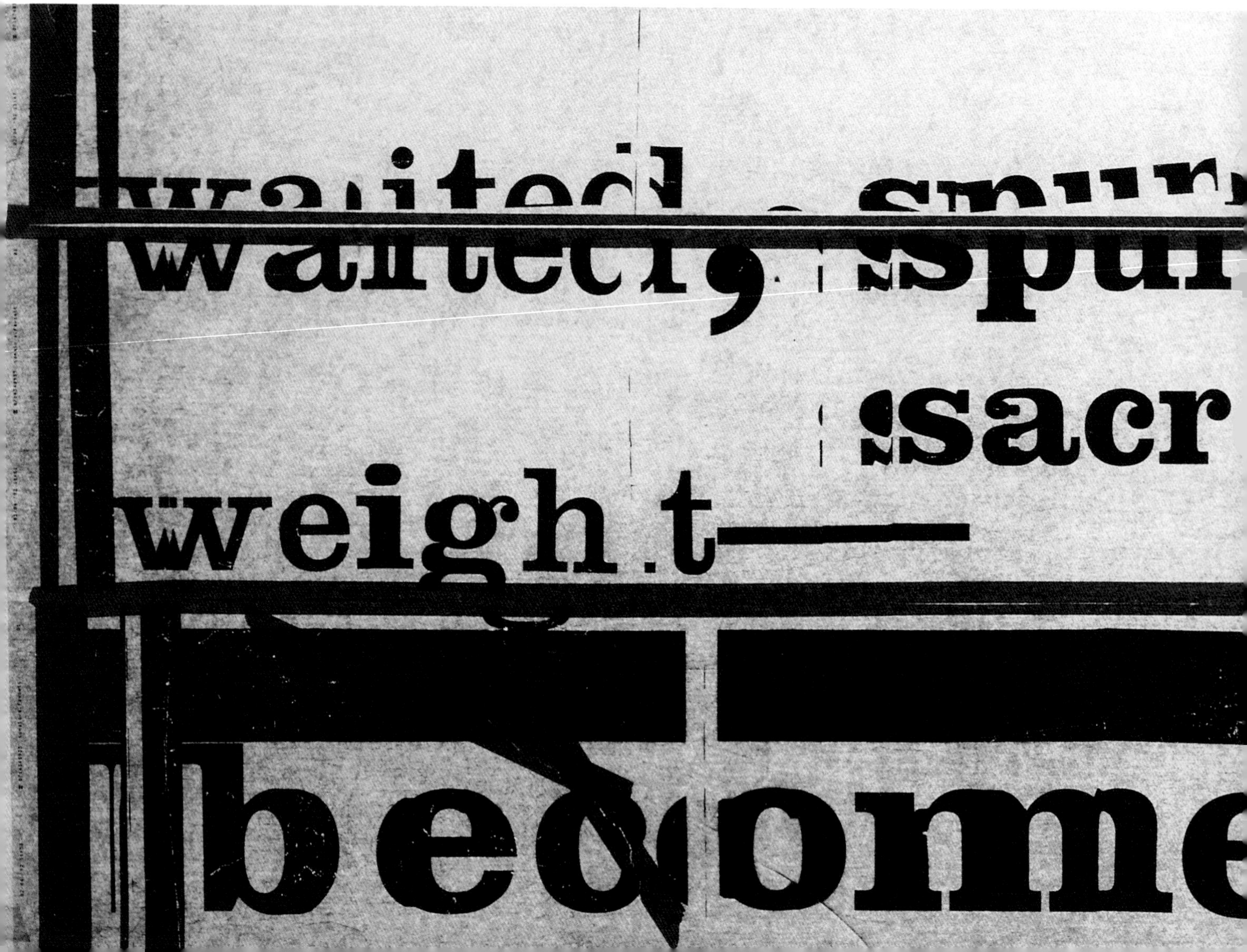

waited, spur

sacr

weight—

becomme

ID
Graham Wood

+44 71 434 0935

date
1993

by hand

Faxes pasted together and then printed as a blueprint.

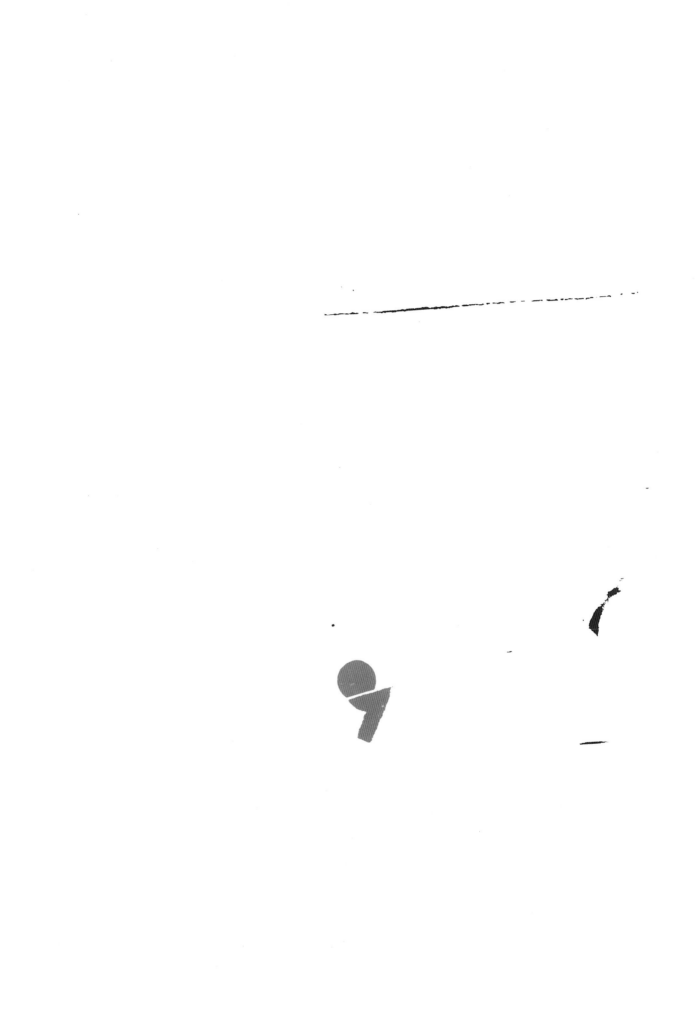

ID
Graham Wood and Phil Baines

+44 71 434 0935

date
1992

by hand

Detail from the poster for "Catholic", an exhibition of typography from Central Saint Martins College of Art and Design, 1983-1992. The logo was produced by faxing, cutting-up and re-faxing type.

cath
olic

ID
Dirk van Dooren

+44 71 434 0935

date
1993

by hand

Illustrations for _Jetset_ magazine which combined faxed elements and thermal paper burnt with cigarettes.

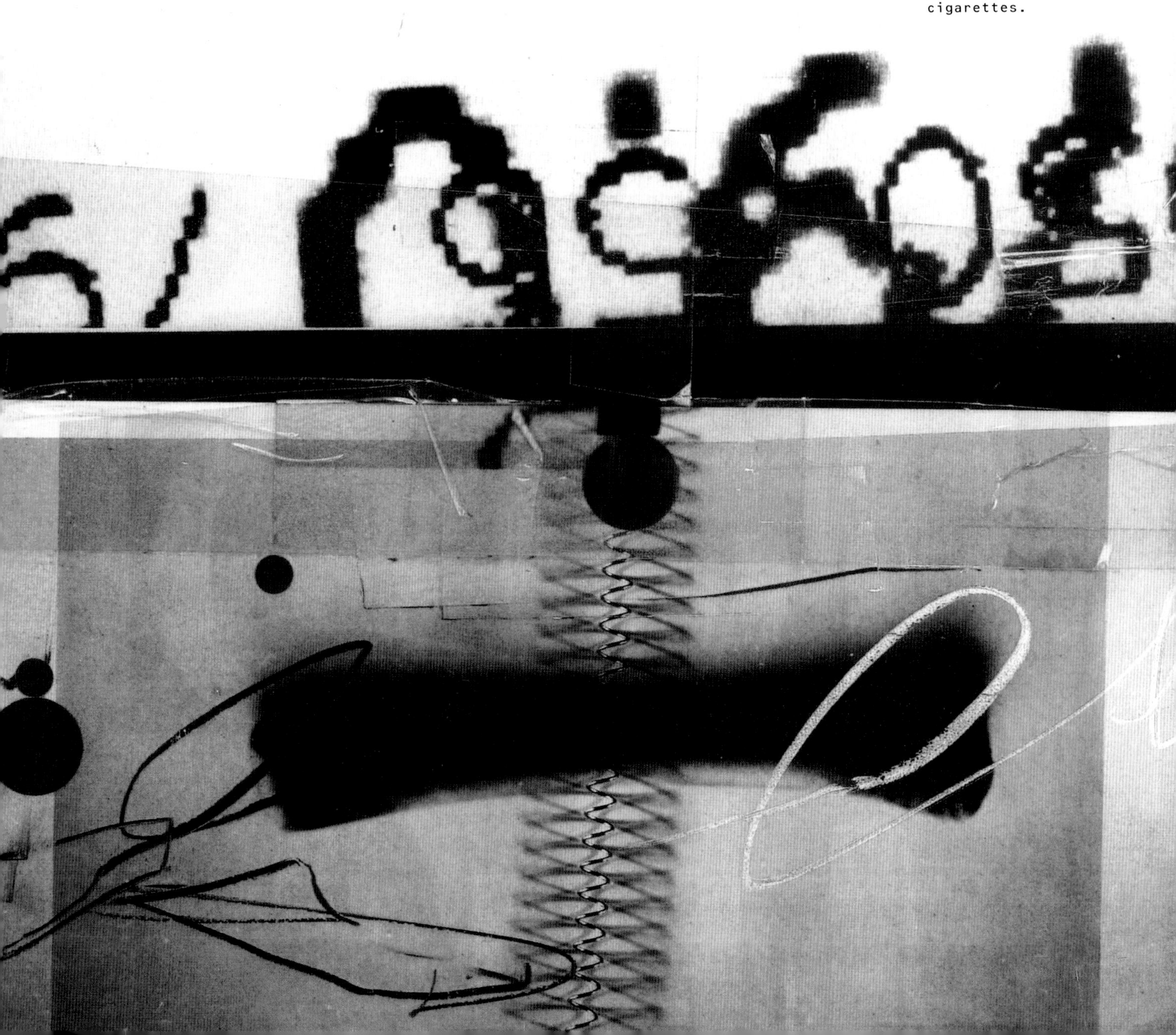

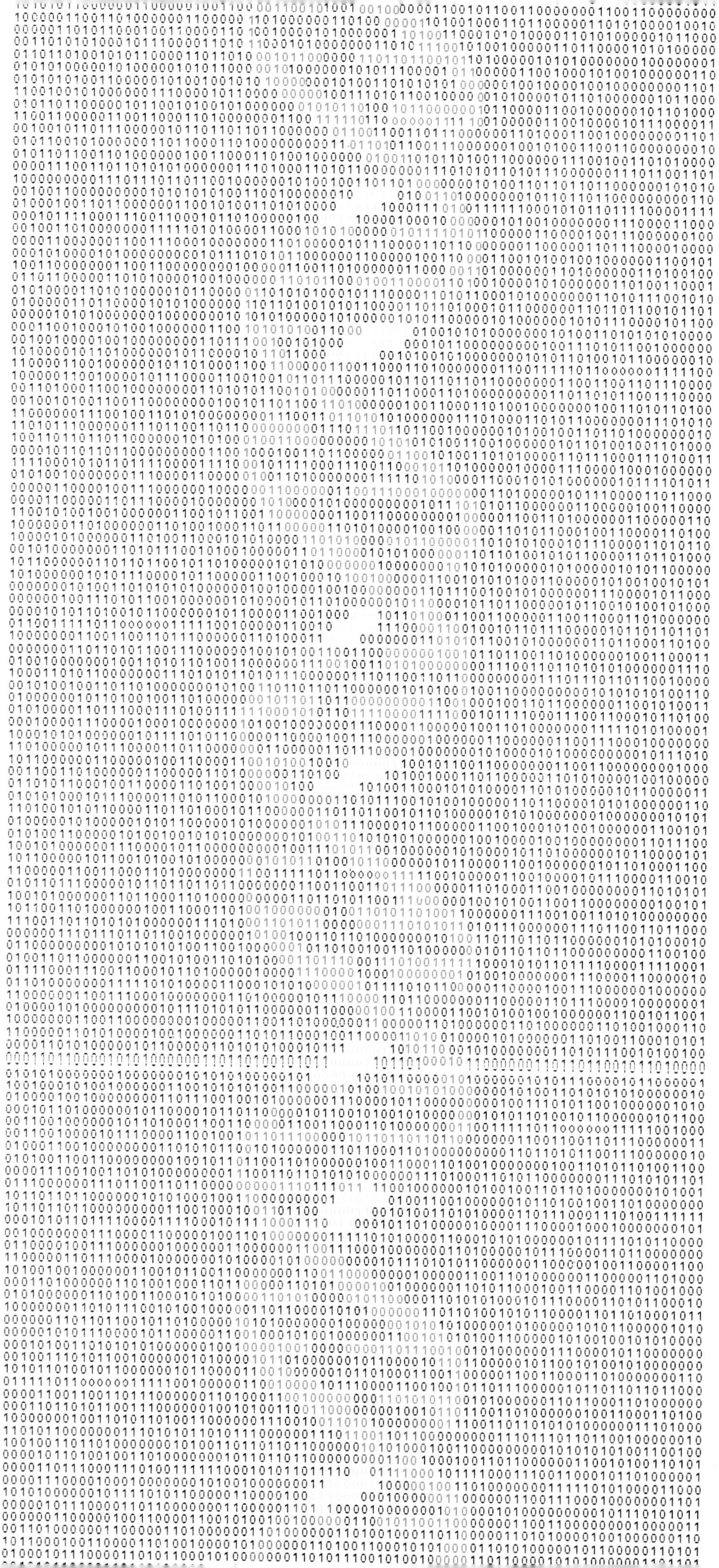

CYANPLATE
MAGENTAPLATE

BLACKPLATE

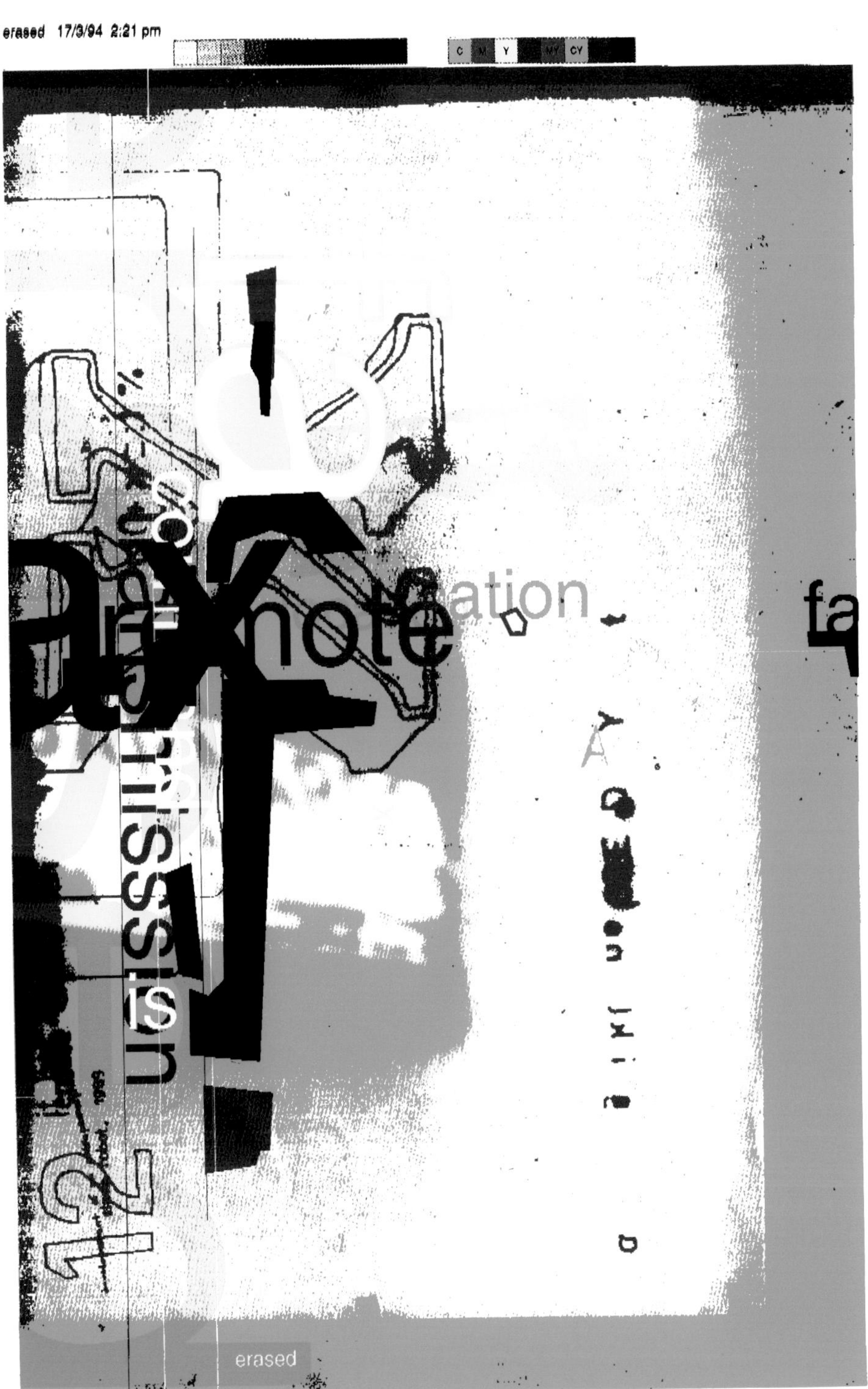

ID
Julian Morey

+44 81 946 0465 and
+44 71 729 5383

date
1994 05 23

duration
00 00' 59"

Faxed by modem for
added clarity.

ID
Carlo Tartaglia

+44 71 225 1487

date
1994 03 17

duration
00 03' 57"

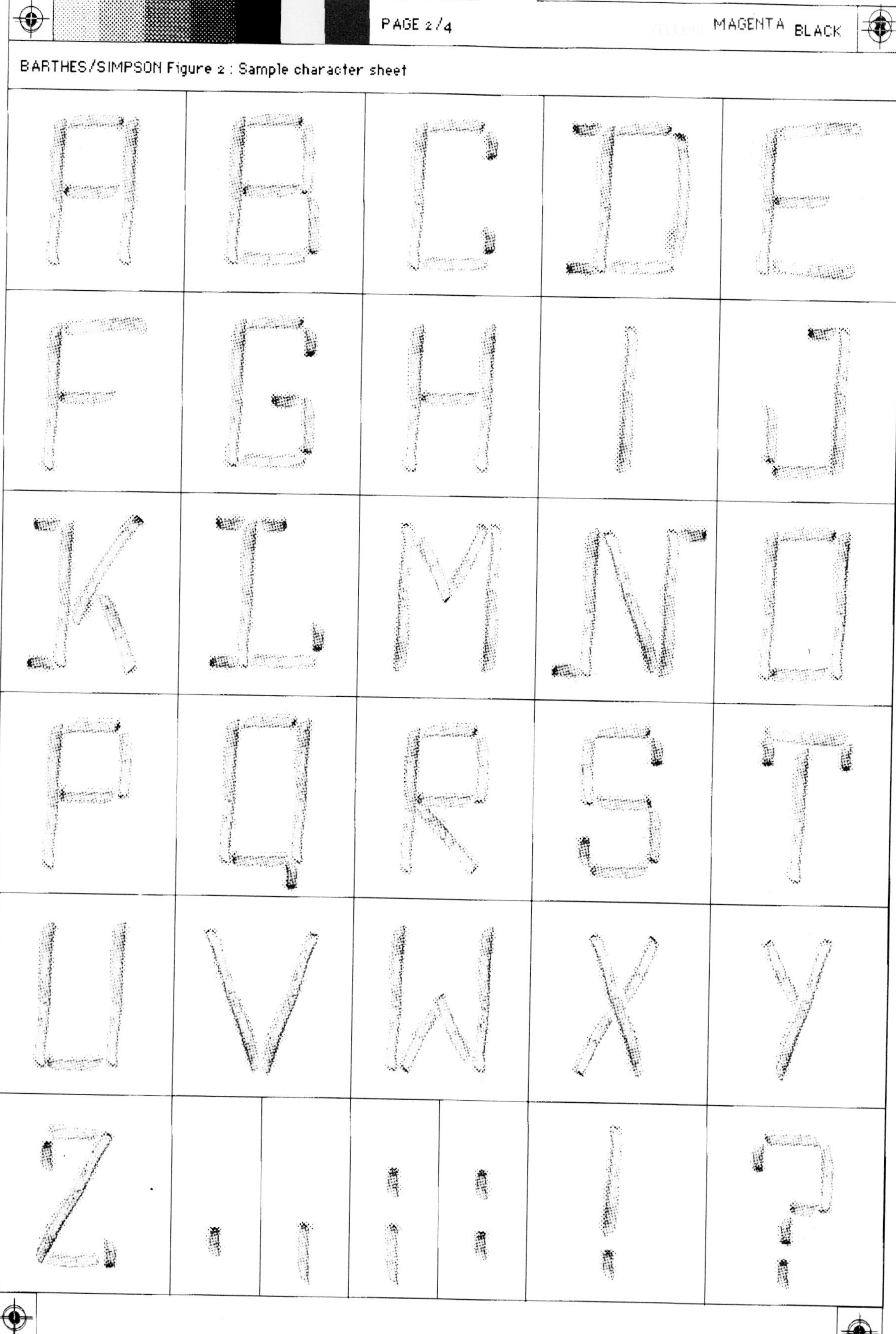
PAGE 2/4
MAGENTA
BLACK
BARTHES/SIMPSON Figure 2 : Sample character sheet

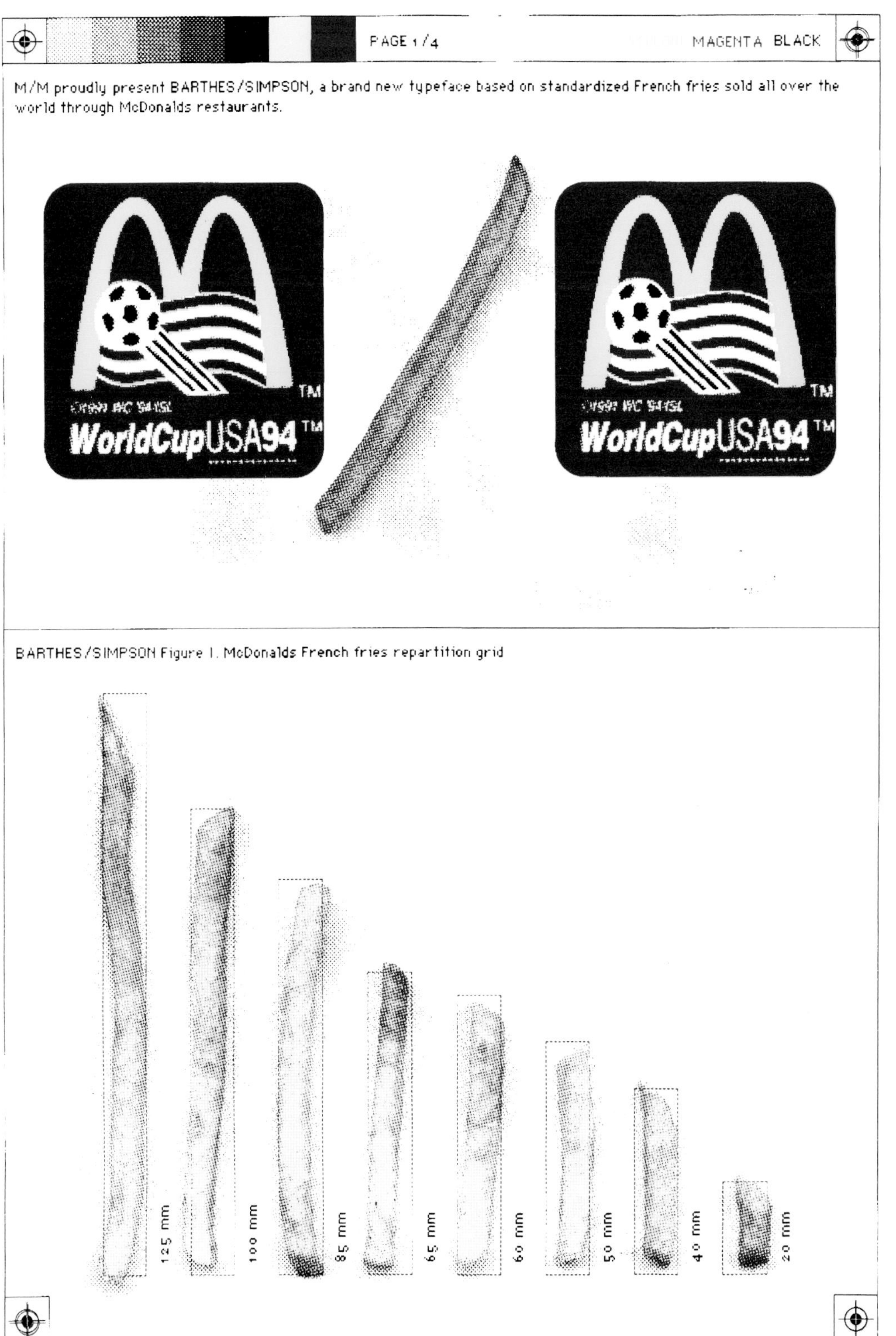

PAGE 1/4
MAGENTA BLACK
M/M proudly present BARTHES/SIMPSON, a brand new typeface based on standardized French fries sold all over the world through McDonalds restaurants.
WorldCupUSA94
BARTHES/SIMPSON Figure 1. McDonalds French fries repartition grid
125 mm
100 mm
85 mm
65 mm
60 mm
50 mm
40 mm
20 mm

ID
M/M Atelier graphique
Michael Amzalag and
Mathias Augustyniak

+33 1 40 36 17 26

date
1994 05 18

duration
00 19' 46"

Talki
e

ngzon

it and
t
is not just being poor
ving a home, it's an issue
try to ignore if they can.
economics
EDUCATION
and
ess are drug
Vereinigung
education is one of many roots of the problem. lack of education leads to
low-paid jobs or unemployment. therefore they cannot afford a home.
one of the reasons why the education system is so poor is because the
teachers are so
poorly paid!
in north carolina, the average school teacher, with a college
degree or a master or a doctorate, earns about $25,000 per
year while a garbage collector earns about $35,000 per year.
in america, the quality of education in the poor or lower class areas is so sub-s
children actually graduate from high school without being able to read. this is
reasons why there are 27 million americans who cannot read or write.
Do you think the
Are people afraid
Do you have any relation(s) to or in Euro
/unification
combination
O
This entrench
conscious with
levision show. it is a written discourse in which we hope to encourage cognitive exercise, so it doesn't use a catchy musi
g to translate the letters, words and paragraphs into structure, relevance, and meaning. during this discourse you can't w
have presented this text as fragments to invite and stimulate your intellectual senses, if these fragments fail to stimula
advent of phot
of film and te
more power. Th
blur the lin
sometimes seem
nearly every british viewer seems to have an opinion about american televisio
america in general. evidence of these attitudes can readily be found in lette
their content.
the authors and designers [of both sides] of this discour
of these two elements is pornography. [Porn] exploits and sells the body.
truth, fashion
bibles and tele
[Porn]
home with the
and other
The Macintosh is the only new
tool that the designer has
his/her arsenal of
syntactic toys and to
ignore its potential is to
cut yourself off from the
opinion and of
[Porn] is any representation of erotic
[Porn] is specifically aimed to cause

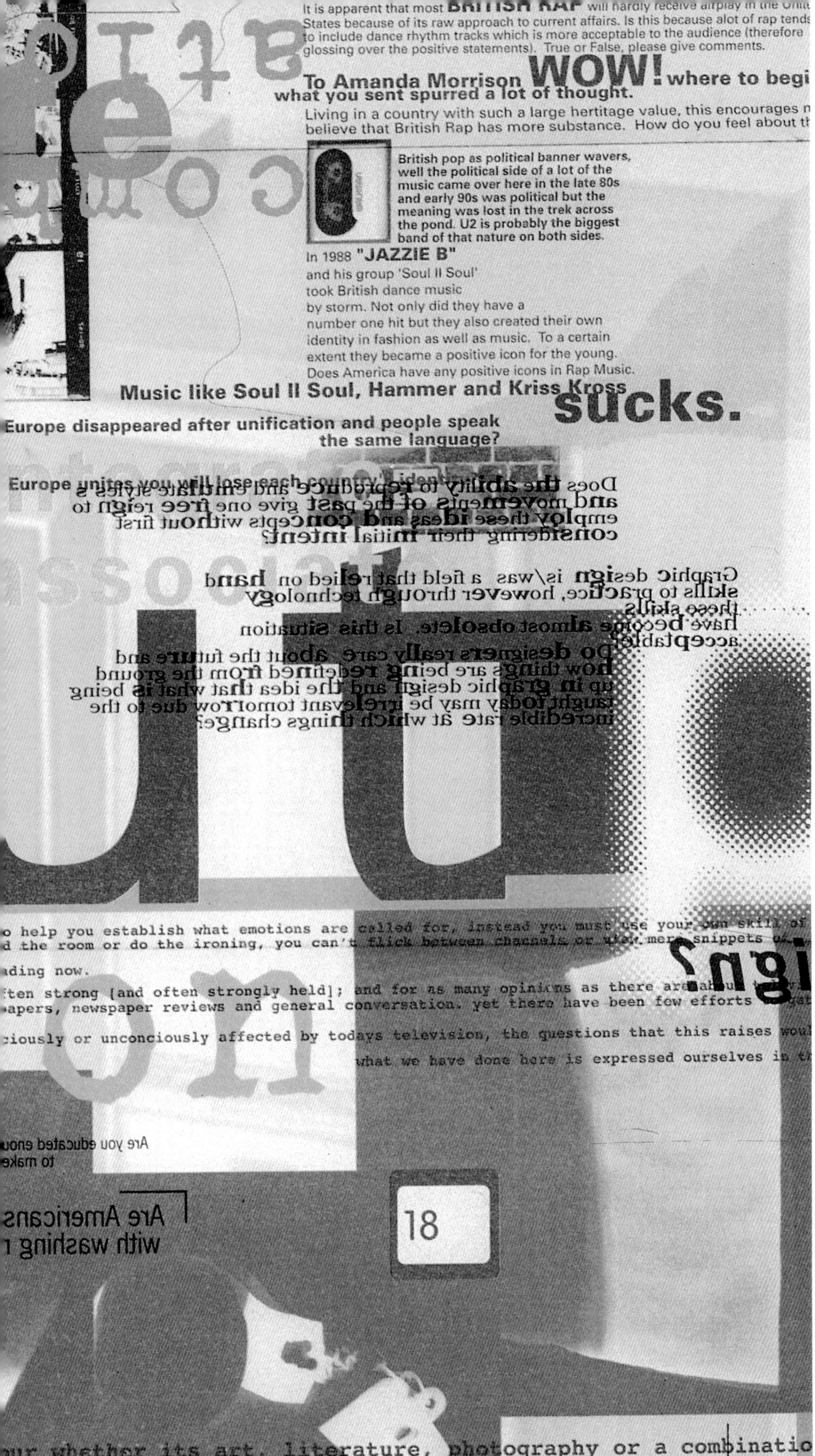

It is apparent that most BRITISH RAP will hardly receive airplay in the United States because of its raw approach to current affairs. Is this because alot of rap tends to include dance rhythm tracks which is more acceptable to the audience (therefore glossing over the positive statements). True or False, please give comments.
To Amanda Morrison WOW! where to begi
what you sent spurred a lot of thought.
British pop as political banner wavers, well the political side of a lot of the music came over here in the late 80s and early 90s was political but the meaning was lost in the trek across the pond. U2 is probably the biggest band of that nature on both sides.
In 1988 "JAZZIE B" and his group 'Soul II Soul' took British dance music by storm. Not only did they have a number one hit but they also created their own identity in fashion as well as music. To a certain extent they became a positive icon for the young. Does America have any positive icons in Rap Music.
Music like Soul II Soul, Hammer and Kriss Kross sucks.
Europe disappeared after unification and people speak the same language?
18

ID
Output 4, special international issue. Produced by students from Ravensbourne College of Design and Communication and North Carolina State University.

+44 81 295 1070
+1 919 515 7330

date
1992

duration
over the course of a year and by post

"In an increasingly technological world communication networks have been readily created, bringing together individuals once separated by geograpahical location...Students from both the USA and the UK insitutions participated in a series of weekly seminars with tutors addressing issues raised by an ongoing transatlantic dialogue...only after a sufficient amount of information had been transmitted and discussed via the fax machine, videos and "care" packages, could an appropriate visual language be determined to convey the ideas and information that had been exchanged." Establishing communication networks by Joani Spadaro and Teal Ann Triggs.

stutter

FAX OBSCENITY
FAX CENSORSHIP
FAX SYSTEMS
FAX ANARCHY
FAX SLOGANS
FAX BABIES
FAX PIGS
FAX DOGMA
FAX GOD
FAX MONEY
FAX WOMEN
FAX MEN
FAX CAPITALISM
FAX TELEVISIONS
FAX FASCISM
FAX SEX
FAX RELATIVES
FAX DEAD
FAX ART
FAX DANCE
FAX PHILISTINISM
FAX WIT
FAX VIOLENCE
FAX HAPPINESS
FAX FREEDOM
FAX EVERYTHING
FAX FUCKING
FAX OFF

ID
Robin Cracknell

+44 81 876 0851

date
1994 02 28

duration
00 02' 03"

"To someone who stutters the fax machine has an emotional and spiritual dimension that can never be appreciated by the average fax user. The fax machine is 'the great equalizer' in the sense that a stutterer can communicate as swiftly and as articulately as anyone else. The fax line is far more democratic and forgiving than its oral counterpart, the telephone. For these reasons, the fax is my redeemer, my protector, my potential realised....It is a blessing and a healer and the illustration reflects this."

ID
Anand Zenz

+44 71 793 9598

date
1994 03 12

duration
00 00' 54"

Fax version of a t-shirt by Anand Zenz.

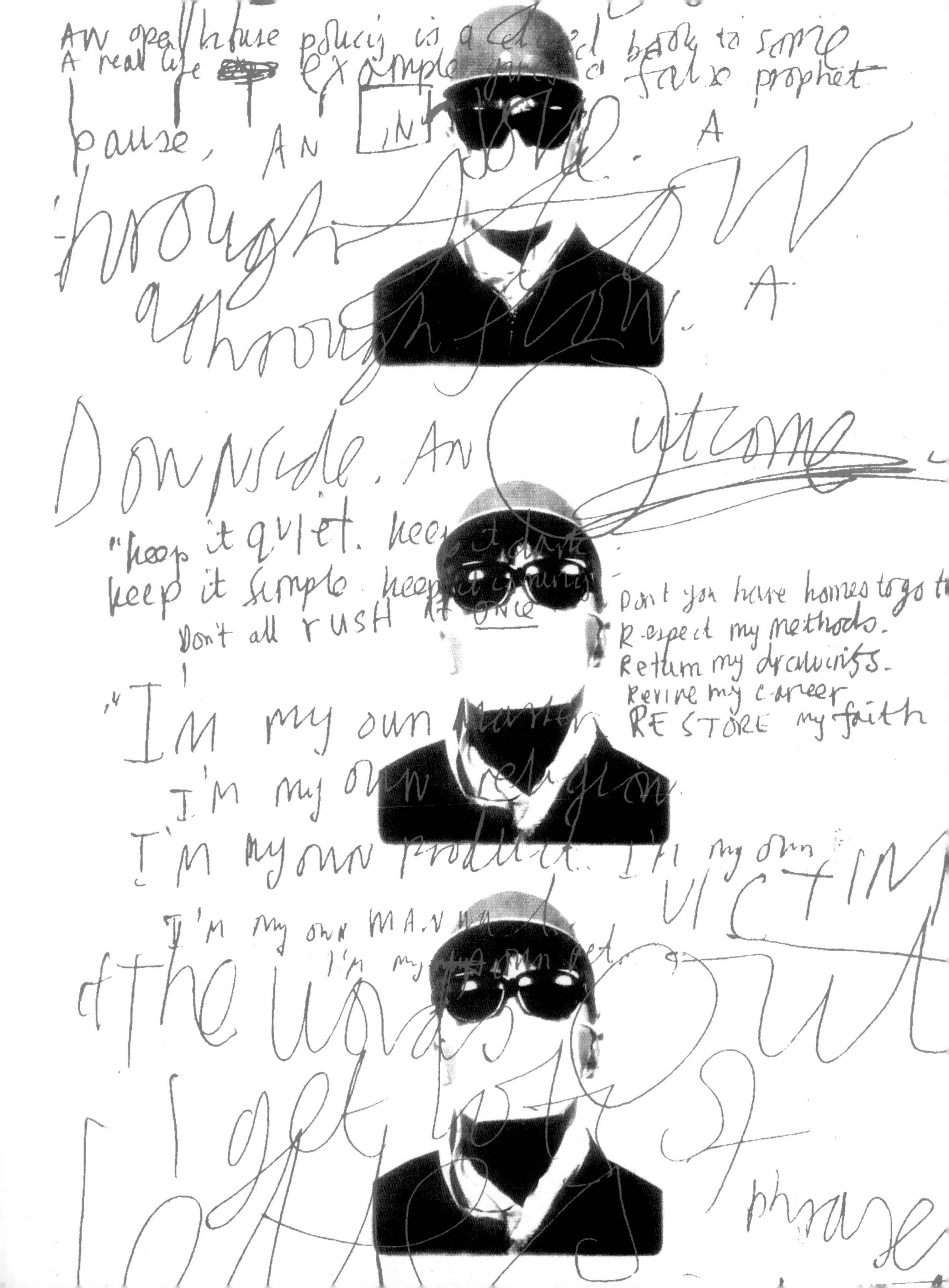

AN open house policy is a closed book to some
A real life example of a false prophet

pause. AN [illegible] A

through a through A

Downside. An outcome

"keep it quiet. keep it dark.
keep it simple. keep it [illegible]
Don't all RUSH AT ONCE

Don't you have homes to go to
Respect my methods.
Return my drawings.
Revive my career
RESTORE my faith

"I'm my own master
I'm my own religion.
I'm my own product. I'm my own VICTIM
I'm my own MANUAL
I'm my own [illegible]

of the [illegible]

I get lost

phrase

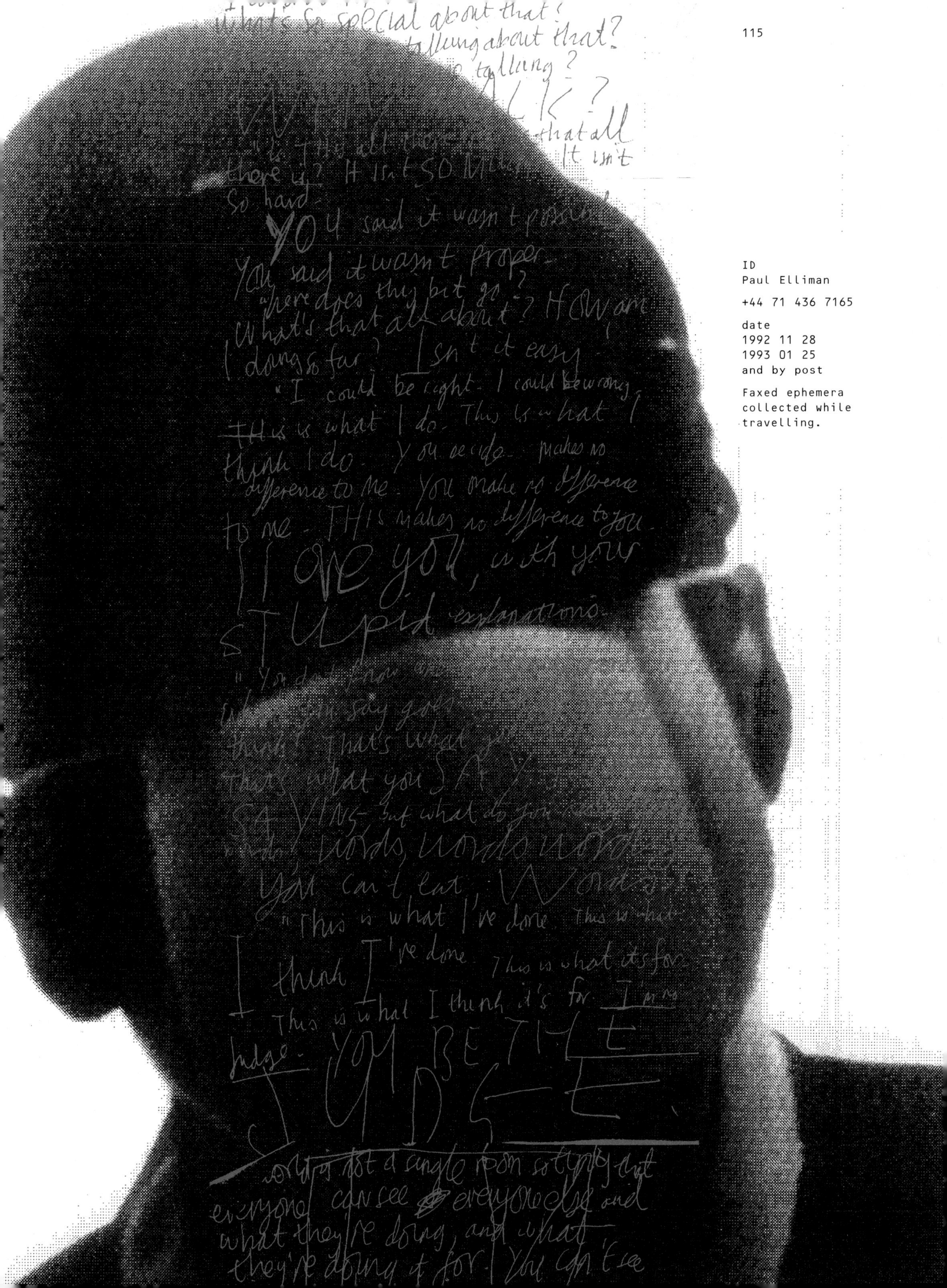

ID
Paul Elliman

+44 71 436 7165

date
1992 11 28
1993 01 25
and by post

Faxed ephemera
collected while
travelling.

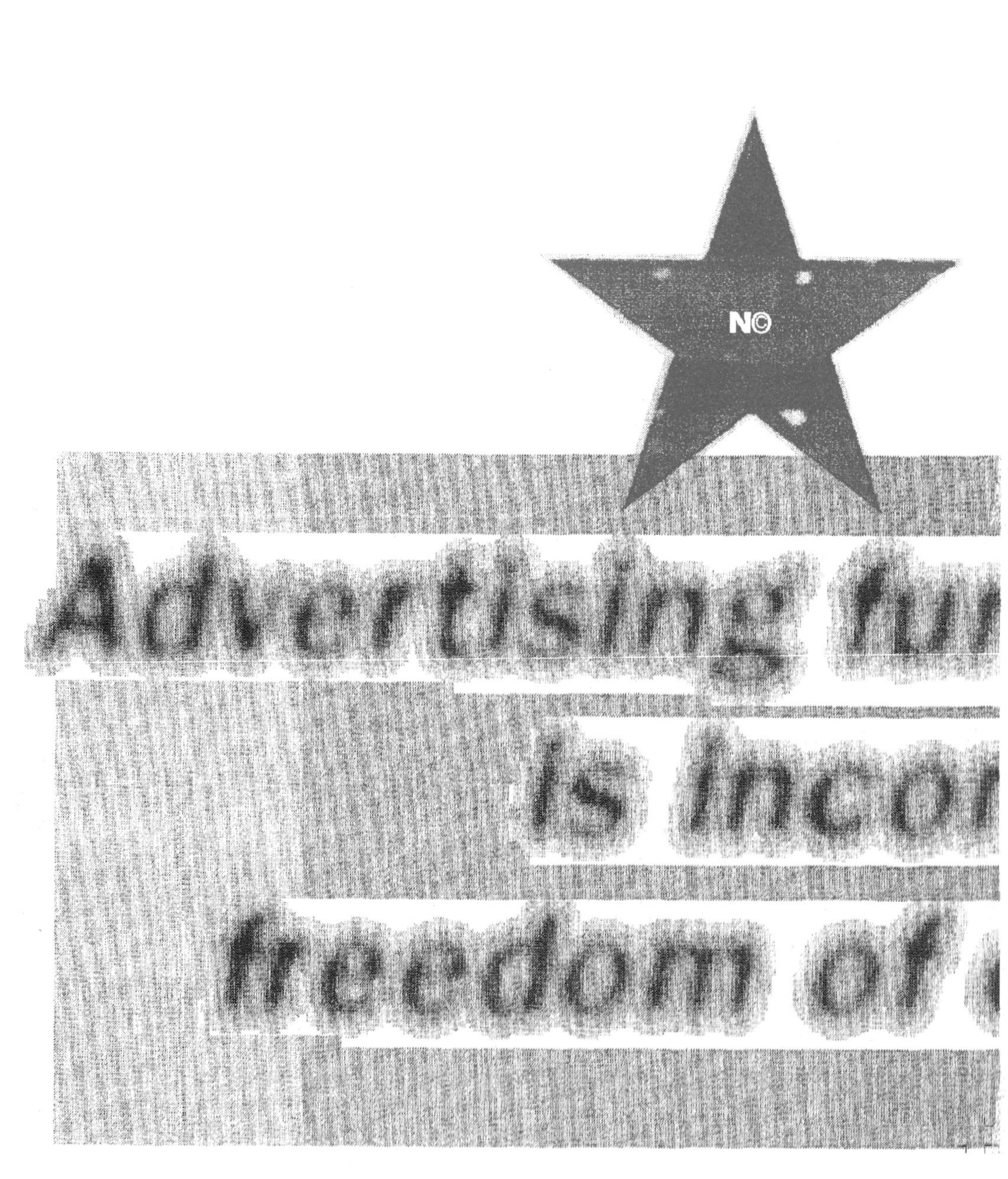
NO
Advertising
is
freedom of

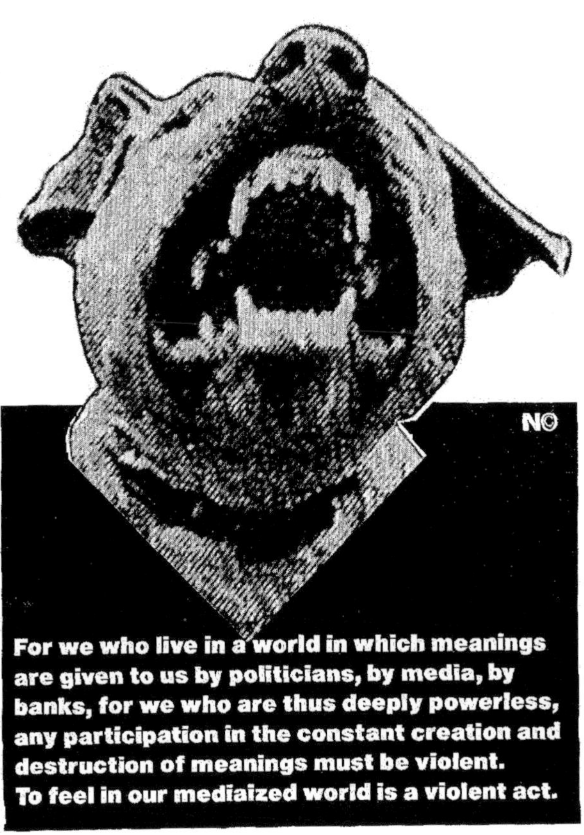

NO
For we who live in a world in which meanings are given to us by politicians, by media, by banks, for we who are thus deeply powerless, any participation in the constant creation and destruction of meanings must be violent.
To feel in our mediaized world is a violent act.

ID
Karen Elliott

+44 81 943 5844

date
1994 04 29

duration
00 38' 06"

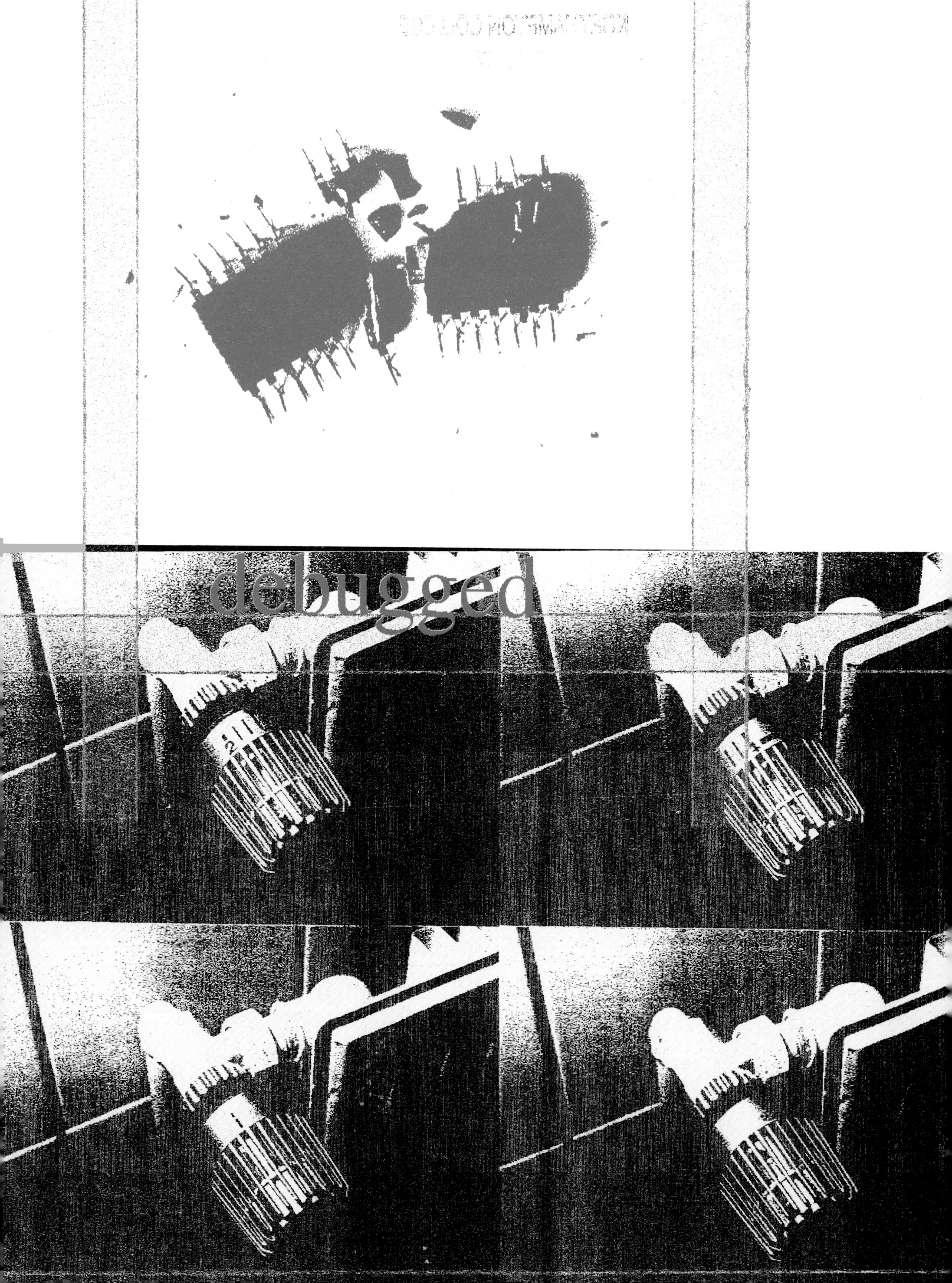
debugged

The Boss

The Cleaner

The Secretary's niece's boyfriend

His Missus The Office Staff

(The Secretary's niece)

The Secretary

The Boss

The Supervisor

Your Best Friend

The Electrician

Your Best Friend

The Supervisor

The Supervisor

The Secretary

The Secretary

Your Worst Enemy

The Boss

The Supervisor

The Boss

(Your Best Friend)

Your Best Friend

The Secretary

The Secretary

The Secretary's niece

The Secretary's niece

The Secretary's niece's boyfriend

The Secretary's niece's boyfriend

Your Best Friend

The Secretary's niece

The Secretary's niece

The Supervisor

Your Worst Enemy

The Supervisor

Your Worst Enemy

Your Best Friend

The Supervisor

The Supervisor

Your Worst Enemy

The Secretary

(The Boss)

The Supervisor

The Secretary's niece

The Secretary's niece's boyfriend

The Boss

The Secretary

The Boss

Your Office Rival

His Mistress

The Tea Boy

(Do you know who's seen it ?)

ID
Wolfgang Schroder
and Computertechnik

+49 4181 36113

date
1994 03 03

duration
00 02' 06"

"Le quattro
stagioni".

ID
Martin Abanyi

+44 81 362 5057

date
1994 05 10

duration
00 00' 38"

TOTALLY

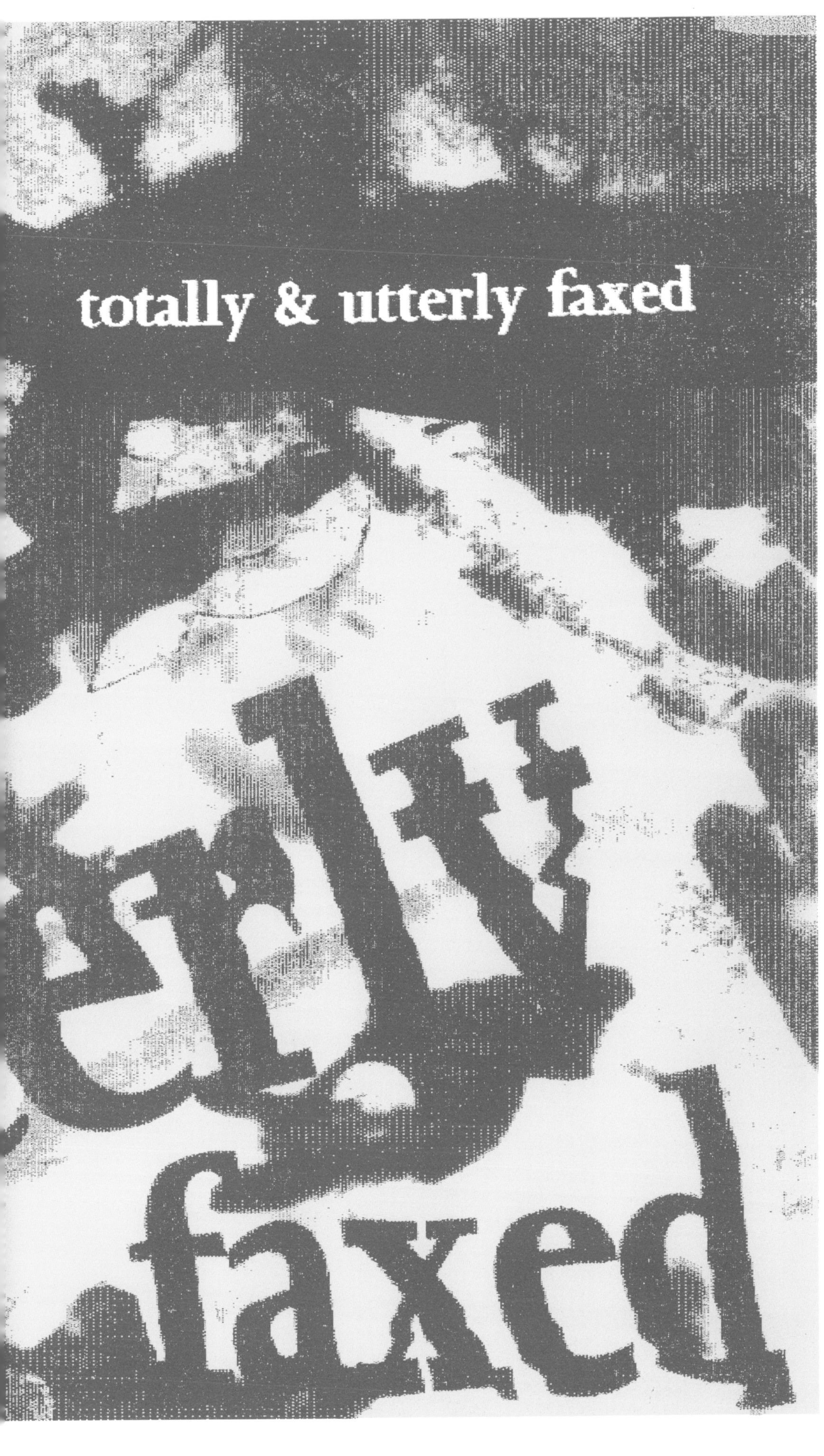

ID
Gavin Pretor-Pinney,
The Idler

+44 71 727 7334

date
1994 05 30

duration
00 00' 58"

It's me !!!

Who are you ?

do you have a name ?

You are not a number

Who are you ?

You are not a number **You are not a number**

Who ?

You are

You have an id

You are real real

You are n

Aren't you ?

You are

You are r

ID
Jen
Middlesex University

+44 81 362 5057

date
1994 06 02

duration
00 03' 29"

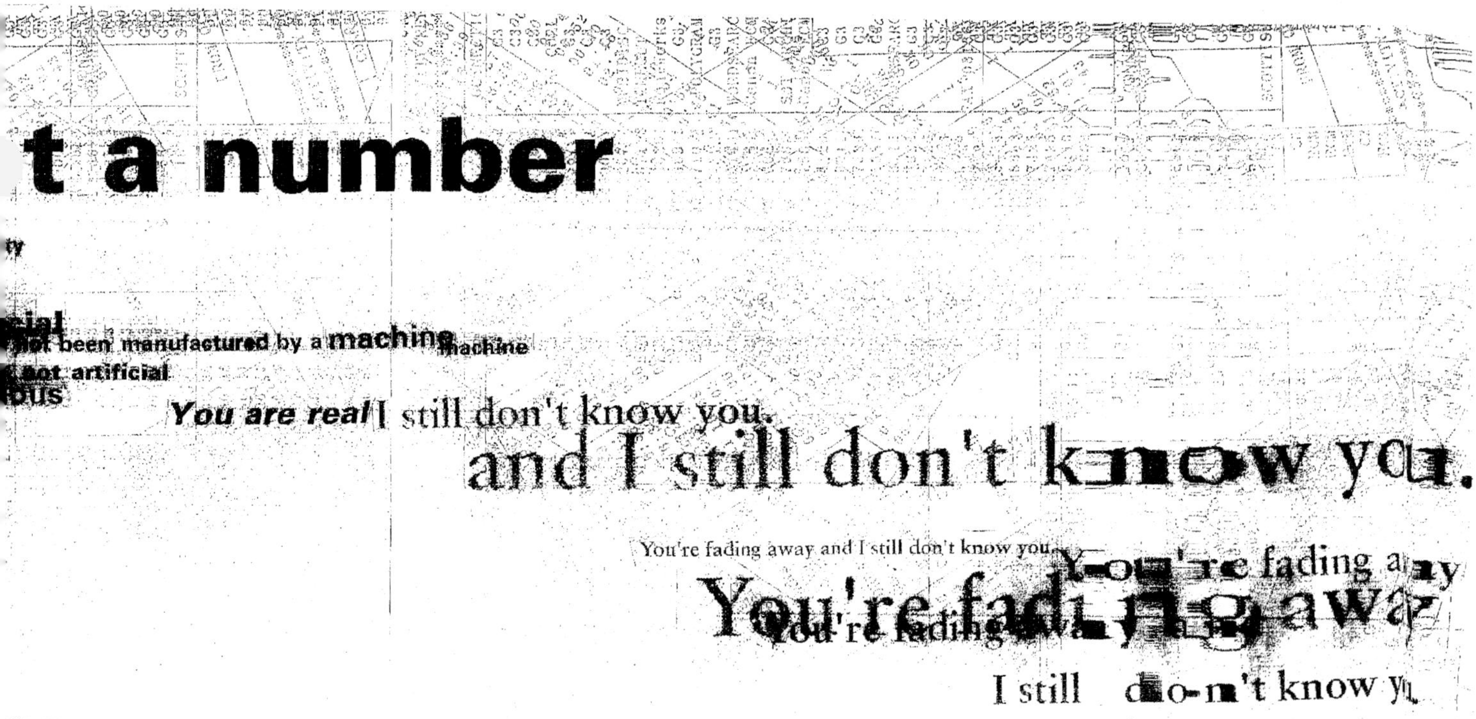

t a number

ty

cial
not been manufactured by a machine machine
not artificial
ous

You are real I still don't know you.

and I still don't know you.

You're fading away and I still don't know you.

You're fading away

You're fading away

You're fading away

I still don't know you

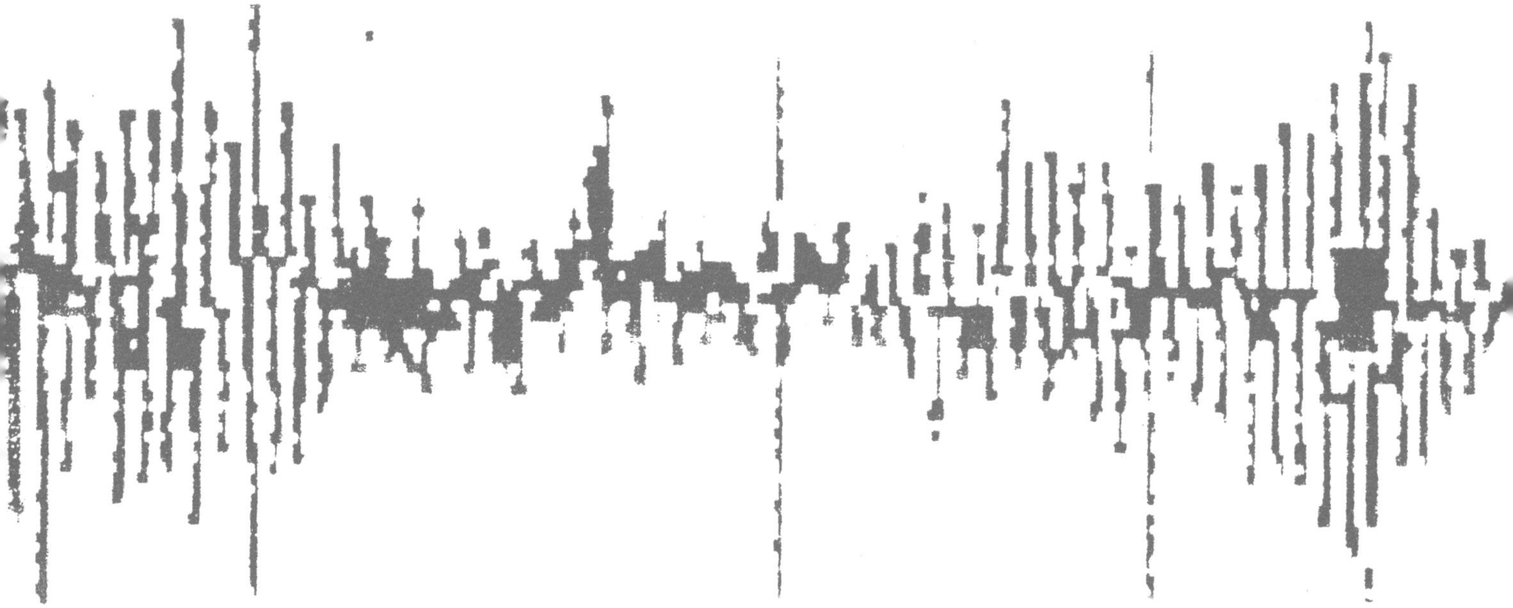

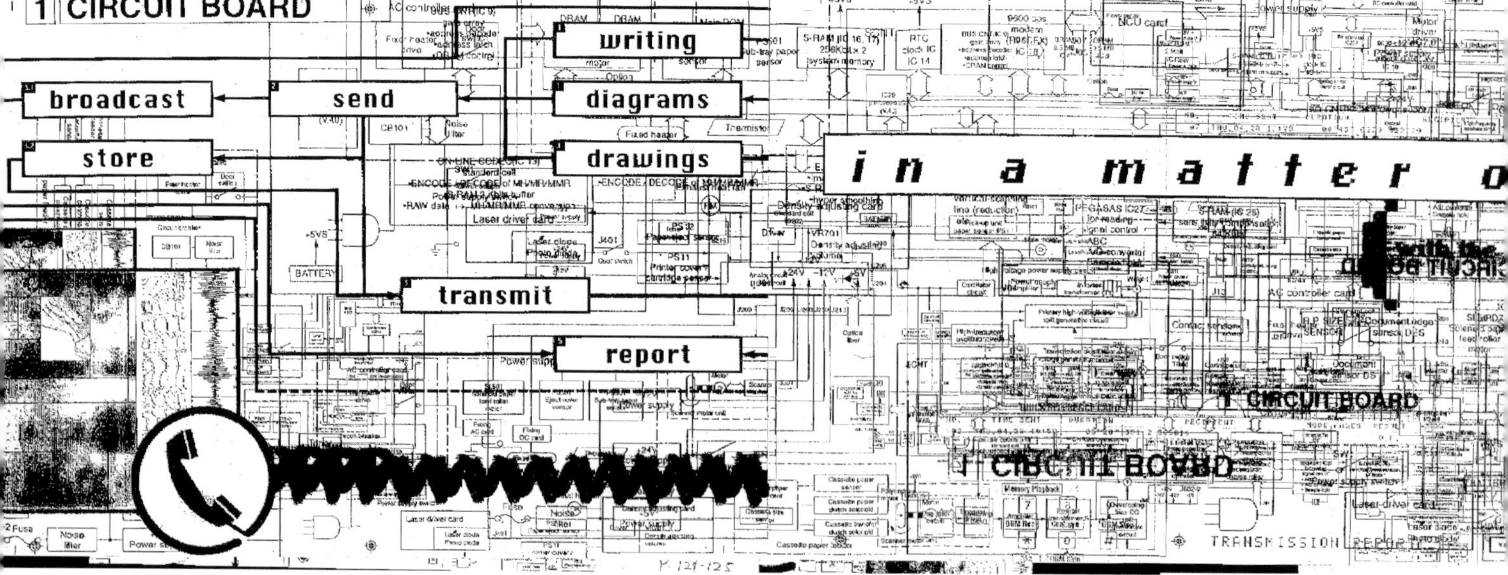
1 CIRCUIT BOARD
writing
broadcast
send
diagrams
store
drawings
i n a m a t t e r o
transmit
report
1 CIRCUIT BOARD
TRANSMISSION REPORT

ID
Mani Norland

+44 81 362 5057

date
1994 05 11

duration
00 05' 46"

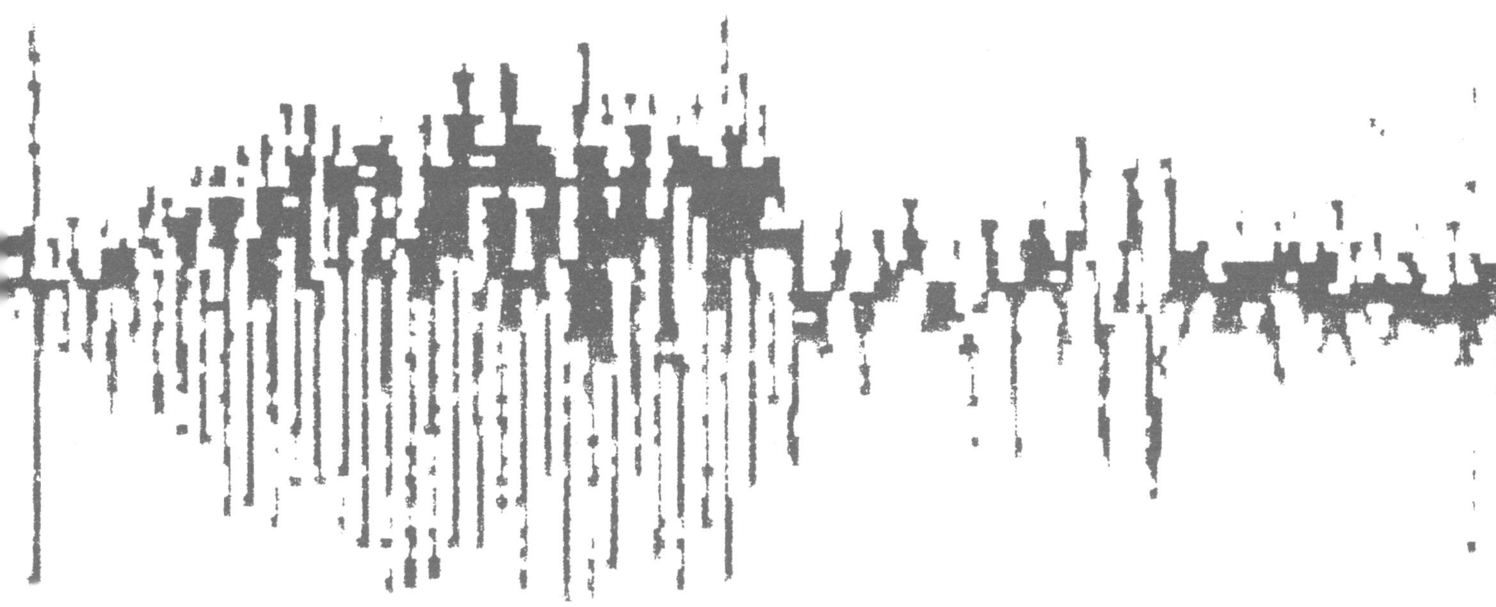

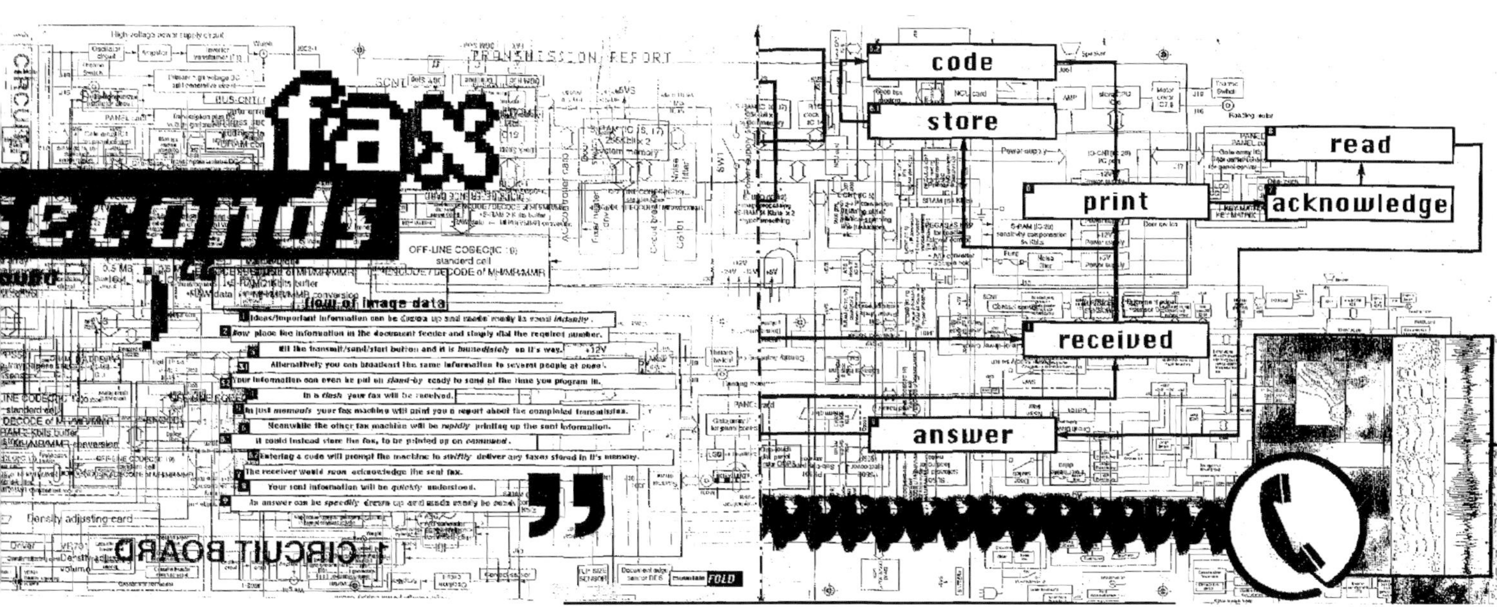

I can be wh...
be - The de...

You dont know me,
I am faceless,
invisible; but for the marks on t...
I could be male or female,
Young or old
I can be whatever you want me t...
the decision is ... Yours!

You dont know me,
I am faceless,
invisible; but for the marks on this paper.
I could be male or female,
Young or old
I can be whatever you want me to be,
the decision is . . Yours!

You dont know me, I am Faceless,
invisible, but for the marks on this paper
I could be male or female, young or old. I can be whatever you want me to be, the decision is yours

You don't know me. I am faceless, invisible but for the marks on this paper. I could be male or female, young or old. I can be whatever you want me to be. The decision is yours.

THE DECISION

You don't know me, I am

YOU

You d

ID
anonymous ("not Clive")

+44 81 362 5057

date
1994 05 12

duration
00 07' 11"

yours.
You don't know me, I am faceless, invisible but for the marks on this paper. I could be male or female, young or old. I can be whatever you want me to be.
The decision is yours.

JUST IMAGINE –

THE OPPORTUNITY TO COMMU

ANYWHERE

WORL

(TRANSMISSION)

can be said, fax instead.

Why?

THE FAX IS MAKING THE WORLD SMALLER

delude ourselves that

we are all growing closer.

What

excited

about

?

JUST IMAGINE –

THE OPPORTUNITY TO COMMU

ANYWHERE

WORL

woul

ID
Clive

+44 81 362 5057

date
1994 05 12

duration
00 06' 47"

TE WITH ANYONE,
THE
N
SIX SE

ECONDS

if the fax is creating a
sub-culture,
then it is one whose members
never meet, speak, hear, touch

SAY?

A VIRTUAL SOCIETY
ENCOUNTER.

there are
1.25 million faxes in the UK
– if you don't have one, you don't exist.
With no-one to hear you,
you don't have a voice.

DID YOU GET MY F

RECEIVE
READ AND DISCARDED.
disposable mediu
disposable message
?

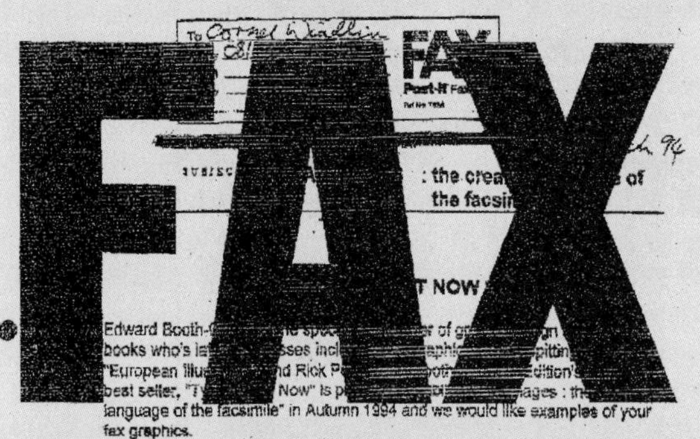

"language of the facsimile" in Autumn 1994 and we would like examples of your fax graphics.

The intention is to provide a record of the graphic and artistic output of the humble office fax machine at a moment in its history when, due to falling prices and ease of use, the fax machine is truly indispensable. Proliferation of fax

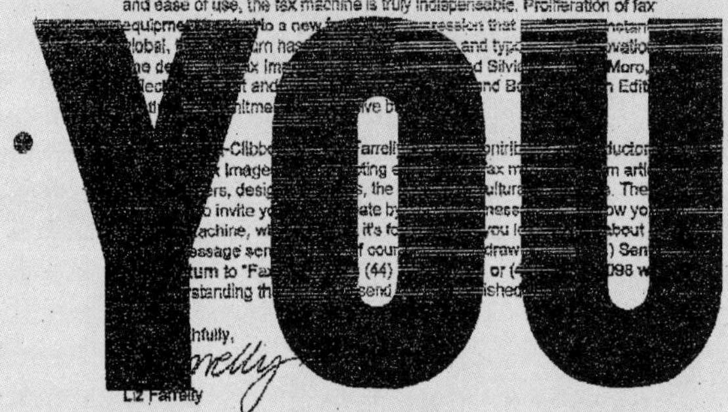

Liz Farrelly

T [44] 71 637 4255 F [44] 71 637 4251

BOOTH-CLIBBORN EDITIONS

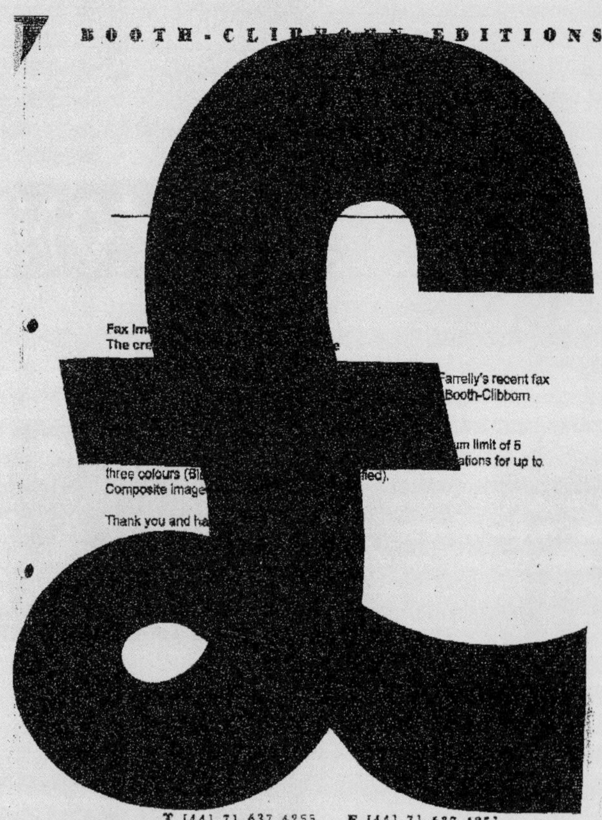

Composite images

T [44] 71 637 4255 F [44] 71 637 4251

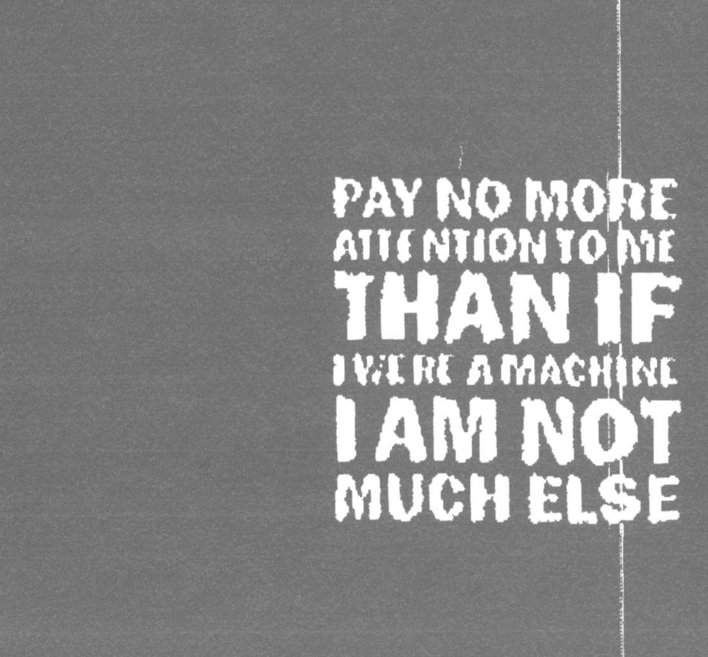

ID
Cornel Windlin

+41 1 272 4301

date
1994 03 14

duration
00 02' 03"

ID
Jon Wozencroft

+44 71 704 2447

date
1994 05 13

duration
00 47' 56"

"This ended up being used as an image in Vagabond (Touch, 1991). Actually it was one of the first things I did on the fax, copying and copying to break down the type into fax-bitmap. The line comes from A Tale of Two Cities by Charles Dickens, which we had used previously on the second Touch audio-visual magazine, Touch 33 (1983).

tente: ZUCCHINA
inatario:
YLSB Data:
08/93 Ora: 15:12
O!!! MA LA COSA
RA POTER ESSERE
RESSANTE
!!! HEHE QUANTI

ente: TITTYLSB
inatario: LILY
04/08/93 Ora:
A CASA?

ente: GI. VI.
inatario:
ESCO 8SX Data:
8/93 Ora: 15:13
ME VA BENE
O!!!!!

CIA E TU????

tente: TITTYLSB
tinatario:
CHINA
a: 04/08/93
: 15:13
E NON MOLTO
ERTA

tente: TITTYLS8
tinatario:
ISSA
a: 04/08/93
: 15:14
NUDA SUL DIVANO
MI MASTURBO

tente: LILY
tinatario: BETA
a: 04/08/93 Ora:
14
IANA DA ROMA CHE
DI BELLO??

tente: BETA 1
tinatario: MANI
FATA
a: 04/08/93
: 15:14
ENO POSSO
AGINARTI.IO SONO
O 1 82, OCCHI E
ELLI SCURI, 30
I

tente: ROSI
tinatario:
TYLSB
a: 04/08/93 Ora:
15
E POI ?? TU CHE
???

15:15
SEI MAI RIUSCITA A
CONOSCERE QUALCUNA
DELLA MSG?

Mittente: ZUCCHINA
Destinatario:
TITTYLSB
Data: 04/08/93
Ora: 15:15
QUANTI ANNI HAI??
EHH??

Mittente: TITTYLSB
Destinatario: ROSI
Data: 04/08/93
Ora: 15:15
IO MI STO
MASTURBANDO DA 10
MINUTI

Mittente: MANI DI
FATA
Destinatario:
TITTYLSB
Data: 04/08/93
Ora: 15:16
16??? MA SON
POCHINI EHH?? !!
DAI DESCRIVIMI LA
TUA FIGHETTA..DAI!!
DIMMI COM'E'??

Mittente: TITTYLSB
Destinatario: BETA
1
Data: 04/08/93
Ora: 15:16
SI' UNA VOLTA

Mittente: LILY
Destinatario:
SCANDALO
Data: 04/08/93 Ora:
15:16 18
ABITI SEMPRE A ROMA
TU?? IO HO CASA
ANCHE A MILANO PER
QUESTIONE DI LAVORO
TU CHE FAI NELLA
VITA?

Mittente: TITTYLSB
Destinatario:
ZUCCHINA
Data: 04/08/93
Ora: 15:16
16

Mittente: LILY
Destinatario:
TITTYLSB
Data: 04/08/93 Ora:
15:16
SI' IN SALOTTO E
TU?

Mittente:
TORTELLINO
Destinatario:
SCANDALO
Data: 04/08/93 Ora:
15:16
..IO?? HEHEHE
CERTO!! PERO' NON
SON MICA UNA LEI
EHH! SON UN LUI..A
CUI PIACCION GLI
UOMINI!!

Mittente: BETA 1
Destinatario: LILY
Data: 04/08/93
Ora: 15:16
IN QUESTO MOMENTO
IN UFFICIO MA NON
LAVORO TROPPO COME
PUOI VEDERE

Mittente: SCANDALO
Destinatario: LILY
Data: 04/08/93 Ora:
15:16
SPETTACOLO... TU?

Mittente: LARISSA
Destinatario:
TITTYLSB
Data: 04/08/93
Ora: 15:16
IO IN

Mittente: FRANCESCO
BSX
Destinatario: GI.
VI.
Data: 04/08/93 Ora:
15:16
..INTERESSANTISSIM
O!! MI METTI
CURIOSITA' !!

Mittente: TITTYLSB
Destinatario: MANI
DI FATA
Data: 04/08/93
Ora: 15:16
NON MOLTO PELOSA
CON UNA CLITO
SENSIBILISSIMA

Mittente: SCANDALO
Destinatario:
TORTELLINO
Data: 04/08/93
Ora: 15:17
AHHHHHHHHH

Mittente: BETA 1
Destinatario:
TITTYLS8
Data: 04/08/93 Ora:
15:17
E TE LA SEI FATTA
POI?

Mittente: ZUCCHINA
Destinatario:
TITTYLSB
Data: 04/08/93 Ora:
15:17 ..16!!
UNA SPLENDIDA ETA'
!! VERAMENTE!

Mittente: TITTYLSB
Destinatario: LILY
Data: 04/08/93
Ora: 15:17
IO SUL DIVANO CHE
MI MASTURBO

Mittente: GI. VI.
Destinatario:
FRANCESCO BSX
Data: 04/08/93
Ora: 15:17
170X70 MRO*

Mittente: ROSI
Destinatario:
TITTYLSB
Data: 04/08/93 Ora:
15:17
ALLORA LO FACCIO
DIMMI CHE FARESTI
CON UNA DONNA???

Mittente: TITTYLSB
Destinatario:
LARISSA
Data: 04/08/93
Ora: 15:17
SIII COME SEI

Mittente: MANI DI
FATA
Destinatario: BETA
1
Data: 04/08/93
Ora: 15:17
SEI UN BEL MORO? IO
HO 35 ANNI, SONO
CASTANA 167X55, E
HO UNA QUINTA HEHE
HEHE

Mittente: LILY
Destinatario: BETA
1
Data: 04/08/93 Ora:
15:18
E SI' ME NE SONO
ACCORTA E COME
MAI??? NESSUNO TI
CONTROLLA??

Mittente: TITTYLSB
Destinatario: BETA
1
Data: 04/08/93
Ora: 15:18
DICIAMO CHE LEI HA
FATTO ME

Destinatario:
TITTYLSB
Data: 04/08/93 Ora:
15:18
STUPENDA!! TI PIACE
CHE TE LO SUCCHINO?
E COME VORRESTI
FARTELO SUCCHIARE??

Mittente: BETA 1
Destinatario: MANI
DI FATA
Data: 04/08/93
Ora: 15:18
AUGURI LE BELLE
TETTE MI FANNO
IMPAZZIRE

Mittente: LILY
Destinatario:
SCANDALO
Data: 04/08/93
Ora: 15:18
FOTOMODELLA CHE
GENERE DI
SPETTACOLO DIMMI
SONO CURIOSA

Mittente: TITTYLS8
Destinatario:
ZUCCHINA
Data: 04/08/93
Ora: 15:18
SOLO UNA VOLTA L'HO
FATTO CON UNA DONNA
SE NO RAGAZZINE

Mittente:
TORTELLINO
Destinatario:
SCANDALO
Data: 04/08/93 Ora:
15:19
..COME AHHHHH? NON
DIRMI CHE NON TI
PIACEREBBE FARTELO
SUCCHIARE EH?? IO
SON BRAVO SAI!!

Mittente: LILY
Destinatario:
TITTYLSB
Data: 04/08/93 Ora:
15:19
E TI PIACE DGT CON
ME MENTRE LO FAI???

Mittente: BETA 1
Destinatario: LILY
Data: 04/08/93
Ora: 15:19
IN QUESTO MOMENTO
NO

Mittente: TITTYLSB
Destinatario: ROSI
Data: 04/08/93
Ora: 15:19
GLI LECCHEREI LA
FICA MENTRE LE
STRIZZO I CAPEZZOLI

Mittente: FRANCESCO
BSX
Destinatario: GI.
VI.
Data: 04/08/93 Ora:
15:19
..MORO? E POI? CHE
GENERE DI VESTITI
USI? CHE COSA TI
PIACE? SEI
ROMANTICO? COME SEI
VESTITO??

Mittente: SCANDALO
Destinatario: LILY
Data: 04/08/93 Ora:
15:19
CINEMA QUALE
AGENZIA HAI A
MILANO?

Mittente: LARISSA
Destinatario:
TITTYLSB
Data: 04/08/93
Ora: 15:19
170X53 BIONDA OCCHI
AZZURRI HO 23 ANNI
FACCIO LA CASSIERA
IN UN BAR

MANIDIFATA
Data: 04/08/93
Ora: 15:19
A TUTTI I MODI
BASTA GODERE

Mittente: LILY
Destinatario: BETA
1
Data: 04/08/93 Ora:
15:20
BE SEI FORTUNATO
ALLORA CHE DGT DI
BELLO ??

Mittente: TITTYLSB
Destinatario: LILY
Data: 04/08/93
Ora: 15:20
SI' FANTASTICO E
GODO

Mittente: MANI DI
FATA
Destinatario: BETA
1
Data: 04/08/93 Ora:
15:20
..GRAZIE!! SON
BELLE!! (PERO' SON
ANCHE SCOMODE
EHHH!! VOI PARLATE
BENE, LE TOCCATE E
LE STRIZZATE E
BASTA!! ..MA
PROVATECI A CORRERE
EHHH!!

Mittente: BETA 1
Destinatario:
TITTYLSB
Data: 04/08/93
Ora: 15:20
LEI ERA UNA BELLA
FICA? RACCONTA DAI

Mittente: SCANDALO
Destinatario:
TORTELLINO
Data: 04/08/93 Ora:
15:20
BRAVO COME?

Mittente: ZUCCHINA
Destinatario:
TITTYLSB
Data: 04/08/93 Ora:
15:20
..RAGAZZINE?? E HAI
MAI PROVATO A FARLO
INSIEME AD UNA
DONNA .. ED UN UOMO
CONTEMPORANEAMENTE?
?

Mittente: TITTYLSB
Destinatario:
LARISSA
Data: 04/08/93
Ora: 15:20
TU LO FAI CON GLI
UOMINI? IO MAI
FATTO

Mittente: TITTYLSB
Destinatario: BETA
1
Data: 04/08/93
Ora: 15:20

Standing with my mom and sister by a stationwagon near my house, my grandmother is a little in the distance and she runs to us and the car, she was the first to see a tribe of American Indians come over the hills and around the homes, stampeding like buffalo, creating dust and holding bows and arrows. Immediately my sister, my mother and I go for the car and drive away, we speed away creating our own dust, leaving my grandmother.

The Indians were chasing me and all the people I am with, almost everyone there had been hit by an arrow, the Indians would not stop chasing us until we were all dead, so I pretend to have been hit and lie face down in the dirt, I held my breath when they came around to inspect the bodies, I could feel them around me kicking the other dead people and shooting the ones they thought may still be alive, I could hear them stabbing the dead with their daggers just because and I remember the sound of sword through flesh.

ID
Anonymous

date
1994 06 22

duration
00 03' 55"

APR-11-94 MON 16:03 CRANBROOK DESIGN P.05

Two men storm into the condominium. Two men, I believe they were wearing black tights, black tops and both had on black ski masks,they storm in to the place, my sister and I are sleeping, now awake. I stand up, the two men had guns and said nothing but I knew they were going to kill my sister, so I stood up and spread my arms to protect her, I felt like a super hero, I was protecting her, I am prepared to take a bullet for her and I did. They shot me. They hit my leg, I felt the bullet in my thigh, the impact did not hurt, but I knew

ID
Jennifer Elsner

+1 810 646 0046

date
1994 04 11

duration
00 04' 09"

"In the performance Dream Cards (1993) I found that dreams I'd had since childhood, that I thought were specifically my own, were dreamt by many people. A sort of Jungian collective un-conscious of dreams surfaced. Dreams communicated from outside the gallery, through the fax machine, work similarly to the act of dreaming. Information we experience during our conscious state, is transmitted into our brain and stored. The gallery space becomes a brain linked to the world and a democratizing of the gallery has occurred."

I cannot see them but I know they are there, the Mafia was approaching the kitchen and about the blow us all away. Bullets were flying and I fall down pretending to be dead. I feel a Mafia guy standing above me, I say to myself don't breathedon't move. A knife starts at the base of my neck and cuts me all the way down my spine, I try not to move but I arch my back as he pulls my skin off of my body exposing my insides. I remember knowing I was going to die, he was going to take my kidneys and I would not be able to survive that kind of infection.

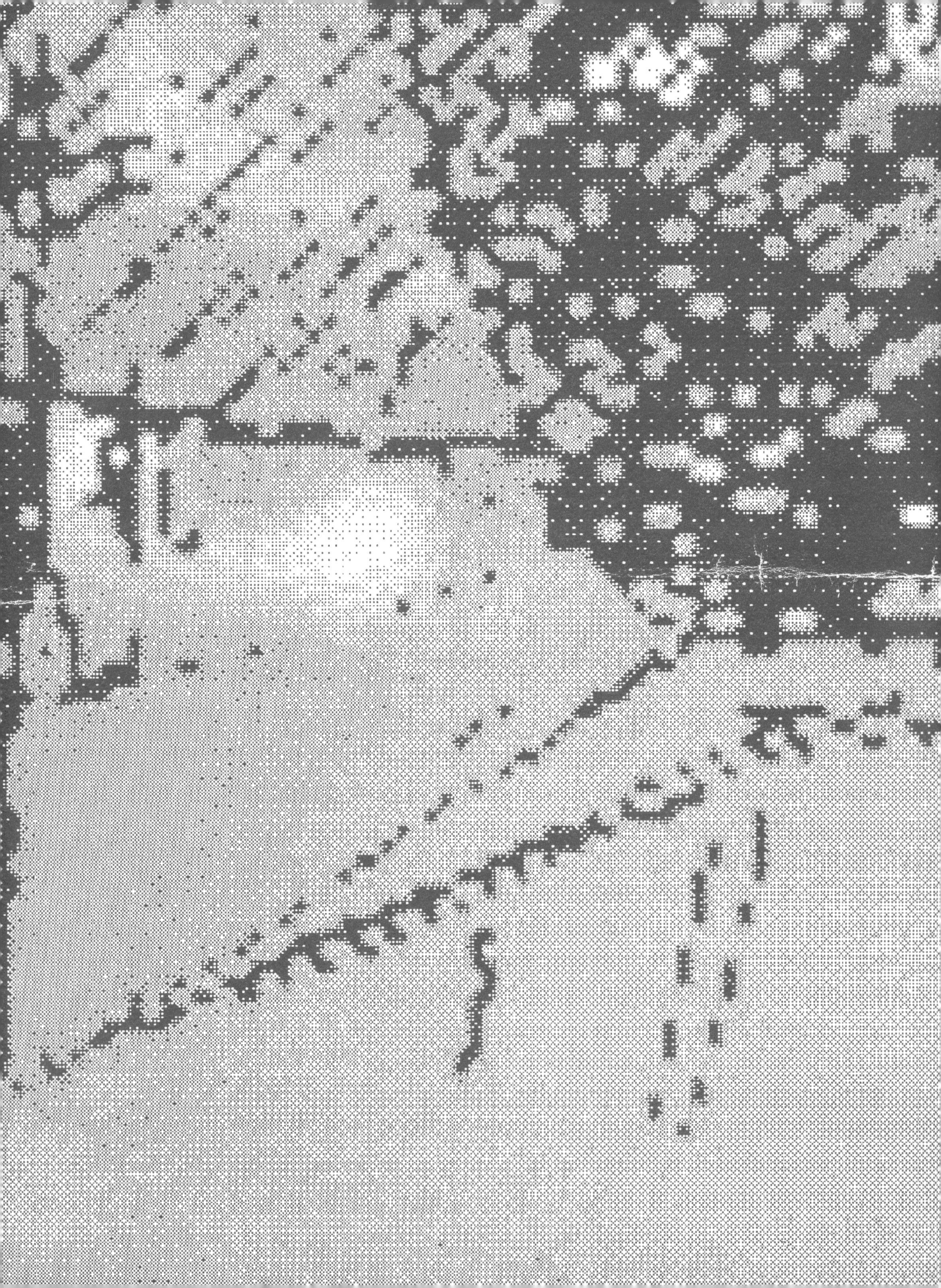

Image4bPalace6.2.94 (Black, 1:2)
The relationship I have with you when you are not here, is my relationship, likewise the relationship you have with me when I am not there is yours.
I guess it is always the case even when we are together, but within the interference patterns set up when we are together, it is difficult to maintain clarity
4.00M
2/10
M Turner '94

ID
Margaret Turner

+61 7 844 4895

date
1994 04 21

by post

Margaret Turner uses a fax machine to output her computer generated work to galleries both within Australia and internationally. The images are usually 2.4 x 1.8 metres and they come off the fax machine in A4 tiles, 64 for each image. "Electronic communication amplifies issues of interpersonal communication which are shaped by the philosophical structures that inform culture. Technology is neutral, the assumptions that drive the users are not". Margaret Turner

INSTRUCTIONS FOR A HEALTHY FAXLIFE.

ONE: USE A WEIRD TYPEFACE IN A SIZE THAT CANNOT BE IGNORED. TWO: WRITE THE MOST IMPORTANT STUFF BY HAND IN A CORNER THAT DOES NOT GET SEND OVER. (3)DON'T EVER USE A COVER. THOSE ARE FOR OFFICE WEENIES. 4. DO NOT WRITE ANY THING REMOTELY CONFIDENTIAL IN A FAX. EVERYBODY READS FAXES ESPECIALLY COOL ONES. USE THIS EFFECT TO START RUMOURS INSTEAD. 5.

DO NOT WRITE A FAX TO SOMEBODY WHO'S GOING TO CALL WITHIN THE TIME IT TAKES TO WRITE. A FAX SHOULD NOT BE LONGER THAN TWO PAGES. AN AMERICAN DESIGNER TOLD ME THAT. SO I STARTED USING THIS SIZE. WHEN YOU USE A WORDPROCESSOR TO WRITE YOUR FAXES: DO NOT PRINT THE NAME OF THE DOCUMENT ON THE PAGE ITSELF. WHOCARES. SO THIS IS A FAX MESSAGE. THIS SHOULD BE QUITE OBVIOUS BECAUSE YOU FOUND THIS PAPER NEXT TO YOUR FAX MACHINE. ONLY REALLY STUPID PEOPLE WOULD WONDER IF MAYBE IT WAS SOMETHING ELSE AND GET CONFUSED. IF THERE IS ANYTHING WRONG WITH THIS MESSAGE THIS WILL NOT BE READABLE. THIS IS NOT A COVER PAGE, THERE ARE NO CONFIDENTIAL MATTERS DISCUSSED IN THIS PAPER. EXPOSING THIS FAX TO DIRECT SUN-LIGHT WILL CAUSE THE TYPE TO FADE, AND DISSAPPEAR. READING IT BEFORE IT FADES IS WHAT WE SUGGEST TO YOU. THE GUIDELINES FOR A HEALTHY FAXLIFE ARE PART OF THE LETTERROR VIRTUAL OFFICE DESIGN IDENTITY, BUT CAN BE REPRODUCED AS A WHOLE WITH MENTION OF ITS SOURCE. EMAIL IS REALLY SO MUCH EASIER AND RECYCLABLE. STUFF GETS ALL OVER THE WORLD FOR A FRACTION OF WHAT IT COSTS TO FAX OR PHONE. I CAN SEND MOVIES OR DESIGNED DOCUMENTS OR WHATEVER I WANT. THAT SAVES A FOREST PER FAX PER YEAR. (ESTIMATE) DO NOT EVER EVER EVER WRITE A FAX IN ONE OF THE 35 STANDARD PRINTERFONTS. IT IS NOT EVEN GOOD-BADTASTE. PLEASE MAKE SURE THAT YOUR OWN NUMBER IS CORRECT. IT IS QUITE A NUISANCE

BODY YOU WANT KEEP
AS A FRIEND. SIX.
LAUGH AT THOSE WHO
SEND FAXES TO YOUR
ANSAPHONE. (7)
FIGHT FAXJUNKMAIL
BY RETURNING THE
PAPER WITH THREATS
ON IT OVER AND OVER
AGAIN. EIGHT* NEVER
ORDER FOOD BY FAX.
9. NEVER FAX YOUR
MOM AFTER NINE AT
NIGHT OR AFTER
DRINKING. TEN:
ALWAYS HAVE ENOUGH
PAPER ON FRIDAY
AFTERNOON.

ONLY FAX THINGS YOU CANNOT TELL SOMEBODY. LETTERROR TYPE AND TYPOGRAPHY, ERIK VAN BLOKLAND, JUST VAN ROSSUM, LAAN VAN MEERDERVOORT ONE F, 2517AA THE HAGUE, THE NETHERLANDS. PHONE 31 70 3605025 FAX 31 70 3106685 EMAIL INTERNET EVB@KNOWARE.NL OR APPLELINK FOL0486 THIS IS REALLY BAD. GET ANGRY AND BE MEAN. WATCH OUT FOR FAXES THAT LOOK LIKE PHONEBILLS, OR INVOICES FOR A MENTION IN THE INTERNATIONAL FAX GUIDE OR EQUIVALENT CRAP LIKE THAT. THE INVOICES ARE FAKE, THE BANKACCOUNT IS REAL OF COURSE. IF YOU'VE GOT TIME TO WRITE A FAX, WALK OVER THE MACHINE, TYPE IN THE NUMBER AND WAIT FOR IT TO GO THROUGH, YOU ALSO HAVE TIME TO GO OUT AND EAT. MY MOM HAS A FAX TOO. THE LENGHT ON AN OLDSTYLE ROLL OF FAX PAPER IS STANDARDISED TO BE USED UP IN A WHOLE NUMBER OF WEEKS, WHERE THE LAST OF THE PAPER RUNS OUT AFTER THE SHOPS HAVE CLOSED. ALSO: THE MOST IMPORTANT PART OF THE MESSAGE WILL BE BURNED INTO THE RUBBER OF THE MACHINE, AND NOT INTO THE PAPER. REMEMBER: THE TELECOM COMPANIES ALL OVER THE WORLD HAVE FIGURED OUT THAT IF SOMEONE SENDS A FAX AND IT DOES NOT GO THROUGH THE FIRST TIME, THEY WILL TRY AGAIN. MOST TELECOMS HAV THEREFORE INSTALLED A SMALL PROGRAM THAT MAKES A SMALL PERCENTAGE OF ATTEMPTED FAXES FAIL DURING THE FIRST HALF OF THE PAGE. ON THE WHOLE THEY MAKE AN INCREDIBLE PROFIT OF IT ALL. SHAKE BEFORE READING.

ID
Erik van Blokland

+31 70 310 6685

date
1994 02 20

duration
00 01' 10"

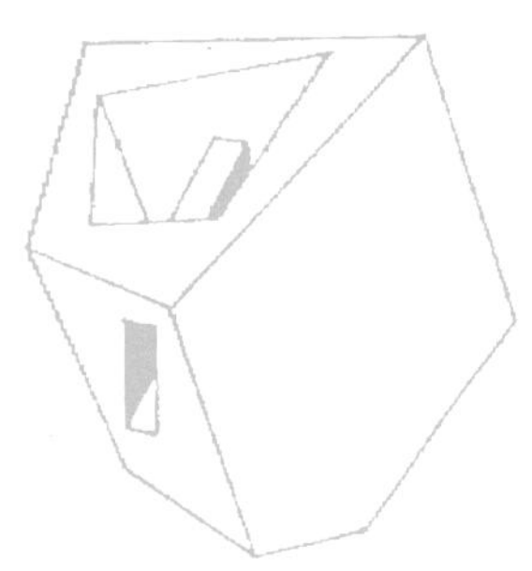

FA

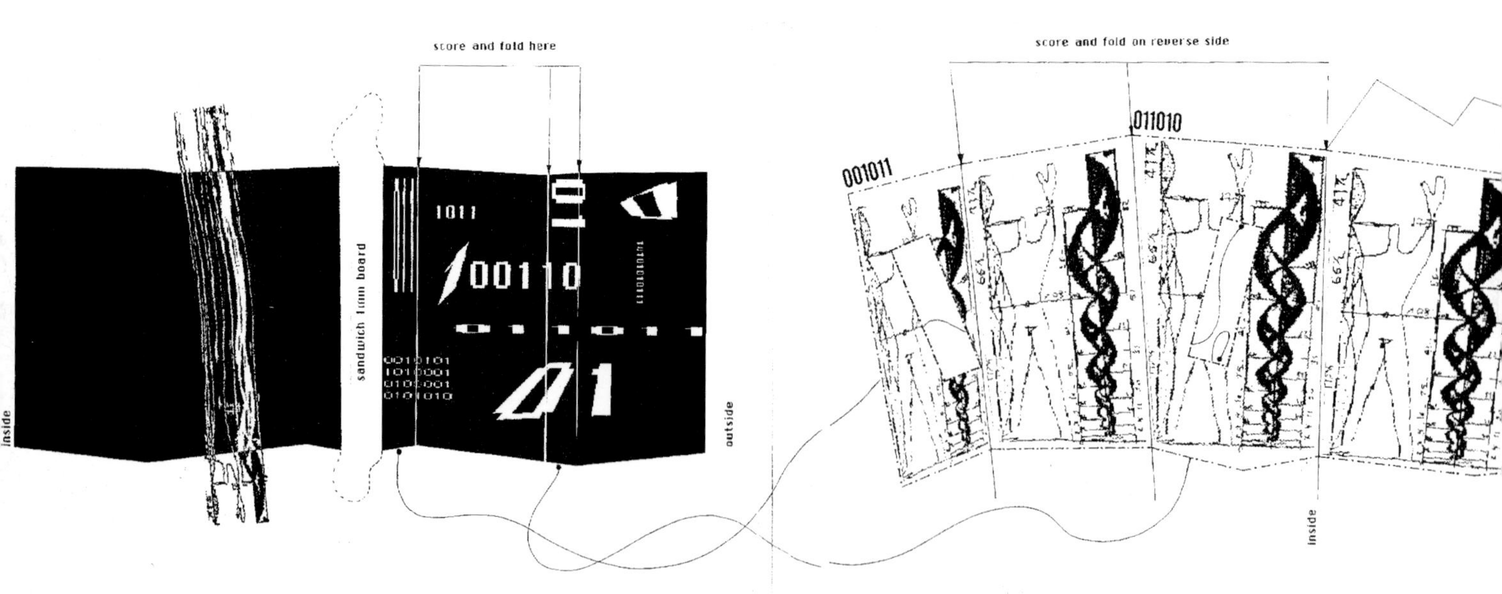
score and fold here
score and fold on reverse side
sandwich 1mm board
inside
outside
inside
1011
00110
011011
01
001011
011010

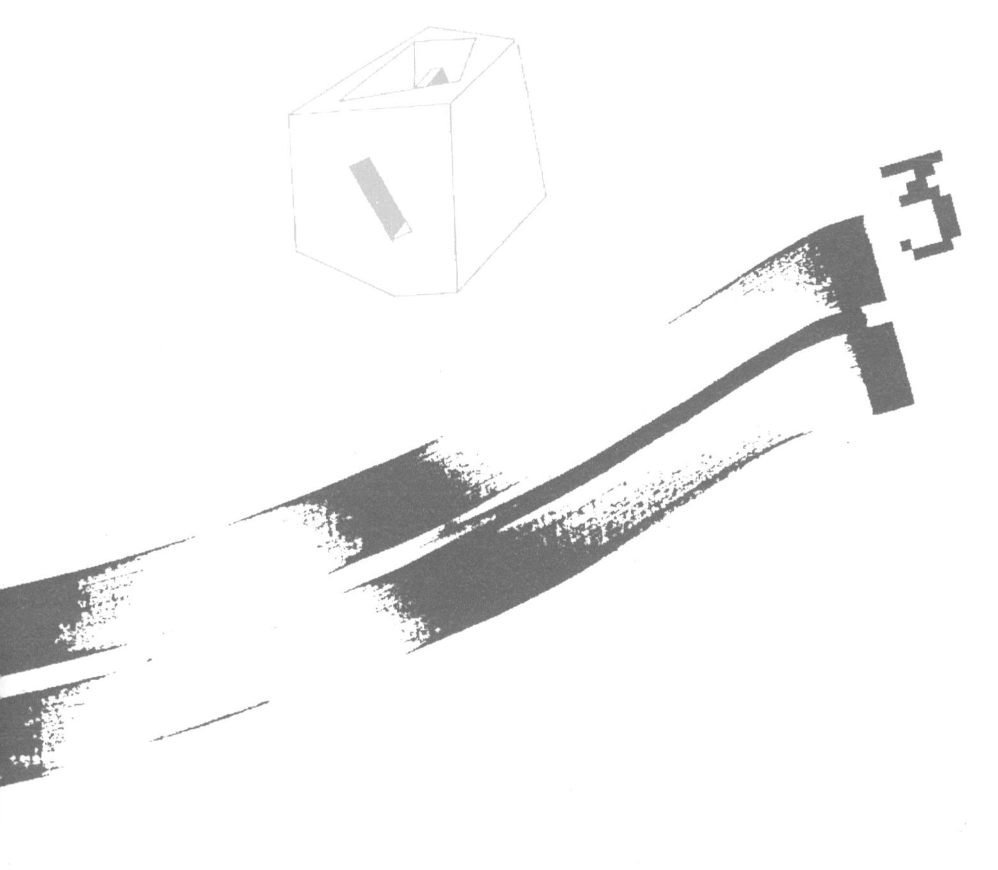

ID
Tony Dunne

+44 71 385 6685

date
1994 05 13

duration
00 05' 26"

"This is a copy of the work I entered for NTT's (a Japanese telecommunications network) 'Museum inside the telephone network' event." A catalogue documenting artworks made with and for telephones and fax machines, both oral and visual, includes Dunne's piece of faxed three-dimensional product design for construction from the faxed original.

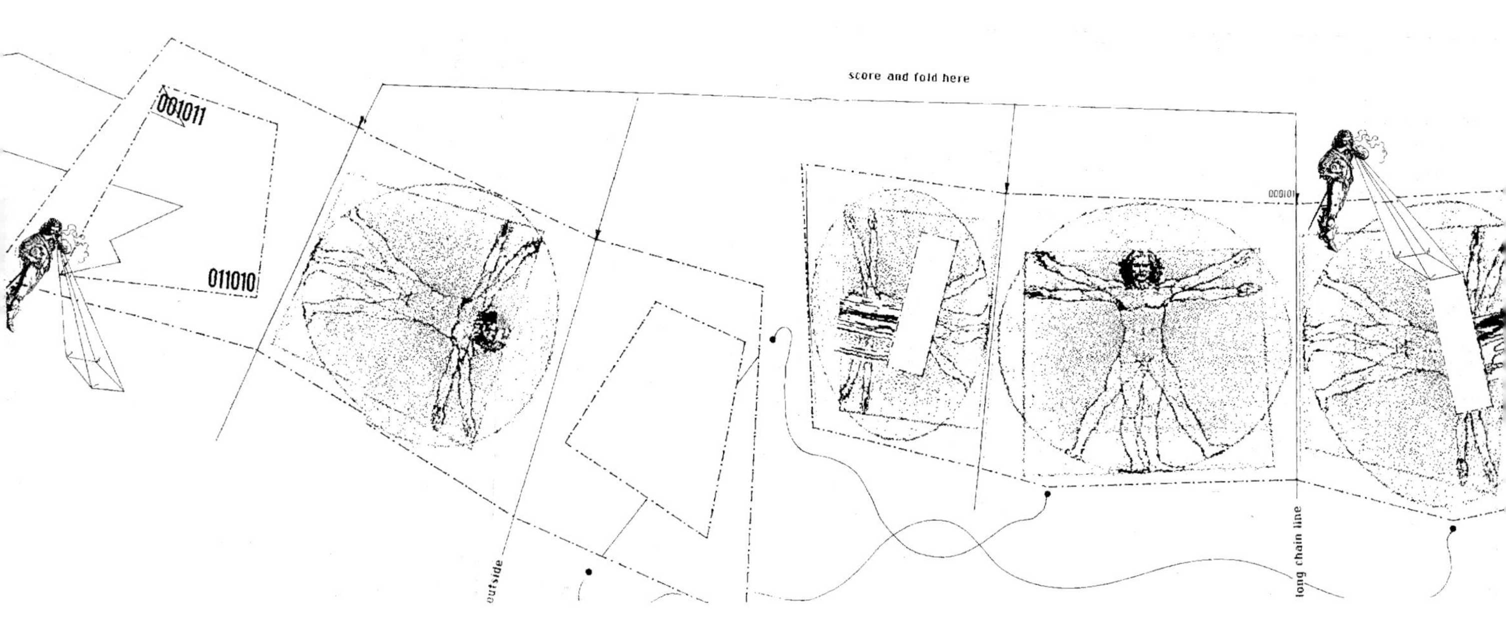

Metas

croll

Graphic Thought Facility
Bayeaux Tapestry

Jason Edwards
The Times

Jon Wozencroft
"Informania" and
"Digital wallpaper"
"This started on the photocopier to create the wave effect, was then reduced to 35% of A4 and copied through the fax machine, blown back up to A4 on the copier, then faxed once again."
Pages from Vagabond, 1991.

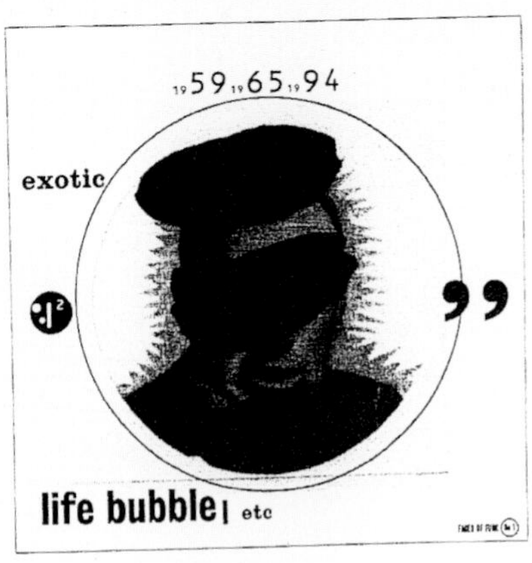
19 59 19 65 19 94
exotic
life bubble etc

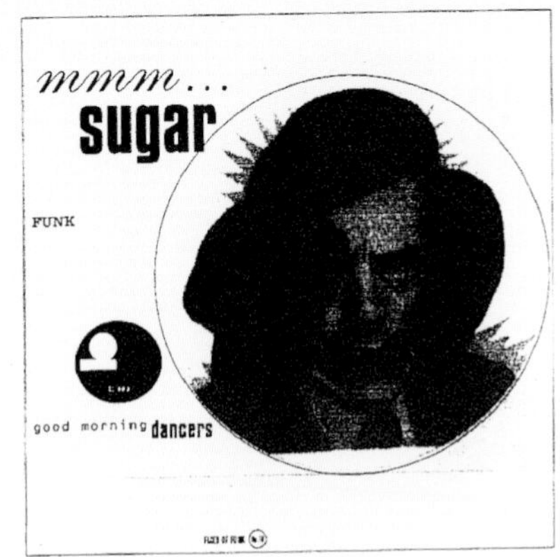
mmm...
sugar
FUNK
good morning dancers

ouch
hey!
845

invisible application
easy to apply
, good

GOOD EVENING
Hey
funk
0.5 mg

only 6 guinea
Funk
fine streets happy beach

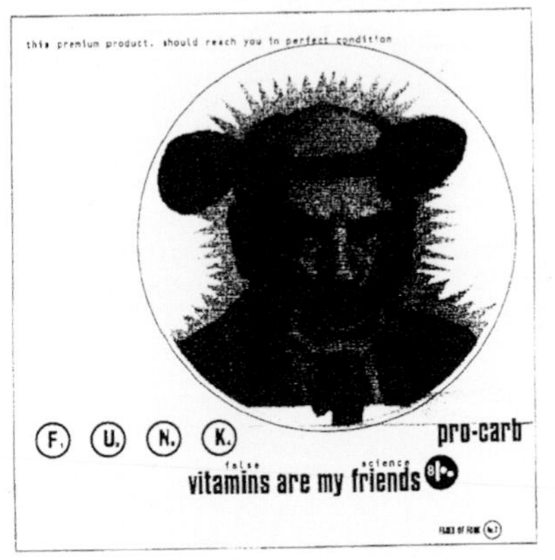
F. U. N. K.
pro-carb
vitamins are my friends

pace
wet
funk
not branded

loafer
CITY/ZIP/STATE
FUNKEN
slow Train

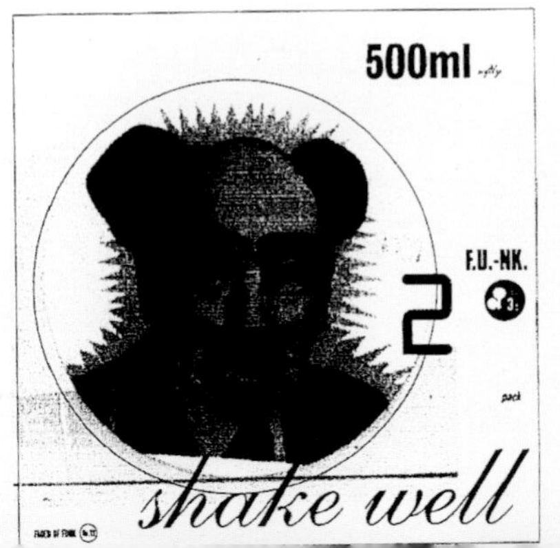
500ml
F.U.-NK.
2
shake well

phunk
LUX fly: chateau

contains
air
square
CALL TODAY
p-funk

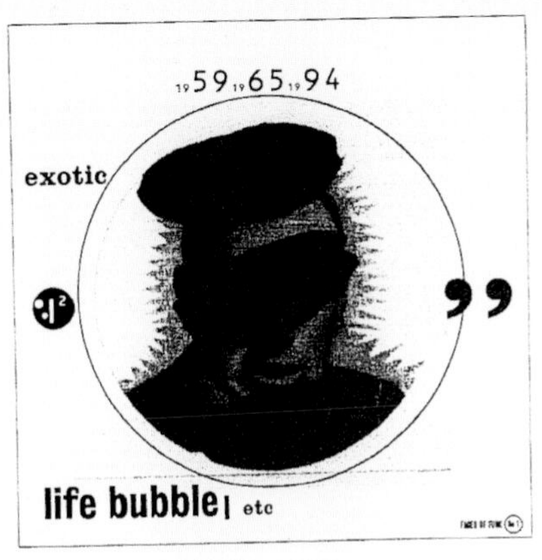

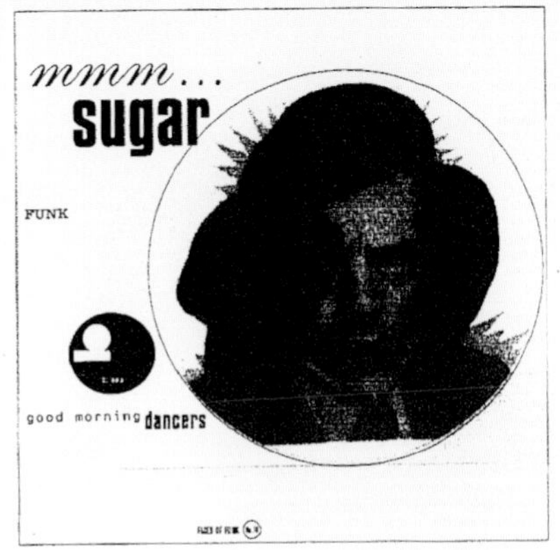

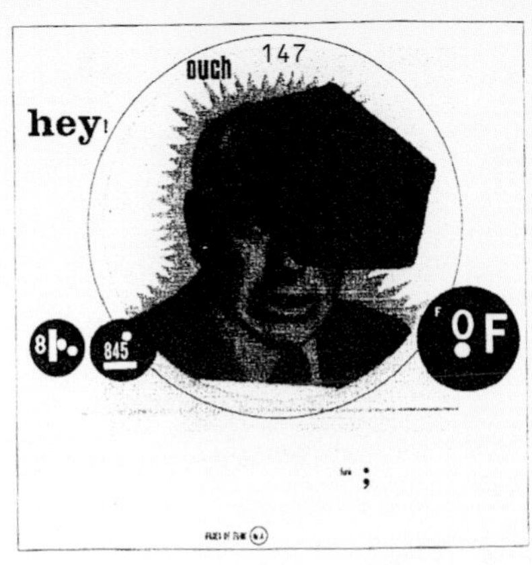

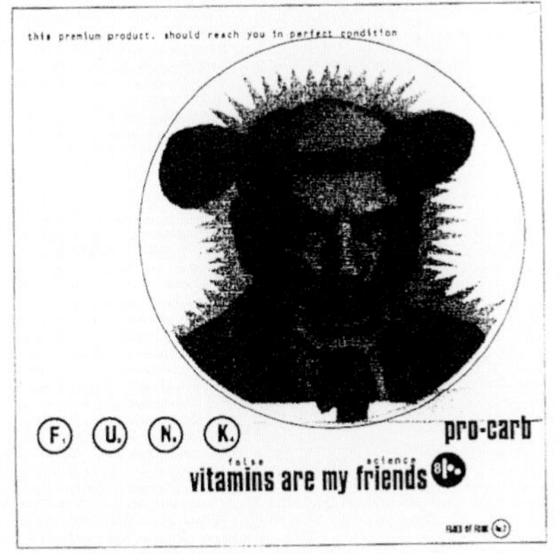

Dirk van Dooren and Simon Taylor Wallpaper faxed to Strive, a bar/nightclub in Fukuoaka, Japan.

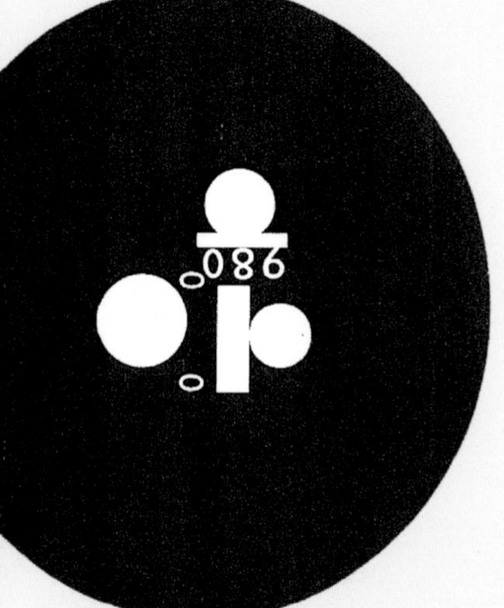

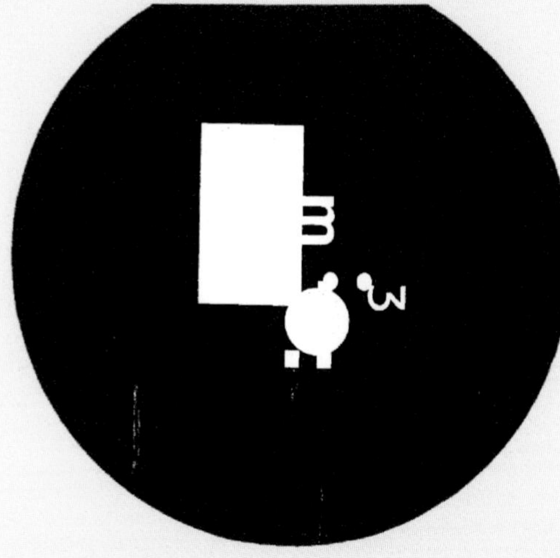

Dirk van Dooren and Simon Taylor Wallpaper faxed to Club Hand, a nightclub in Antwerp, Belgium.

Jason Kedgley
Interference
wallpaper

Dirk van Dooren
Heat wallpaper

WITH LOVE FROM BIG-ACTIVE

50% Extra

WITH LOVE FROM BIG-ACTIVE

50% Extra

Emma Webb and Stefan Bufler
"In the early 1980s fax bugs were being sent around companies in London. The set up consisted of a loop of paper fed through the machine which sent an endless fax. The process uses all the receiver's paper in a matter of minutes. The action of a continuous output from one source reminded us of the printing processes and conveyor belts. Our intention is to use the fax as a machine that will create a product and deliver it at the same time. We want to show that our domestic environment is characterised by mass-produced objects (even the food that we eat). Our source of production is a loop of continuous pattern of two products that symbolise our idea. The roll of fax paper then becomes a roll of patterned wallpaper. We see our project completed when the "fax wallpaper" is used to decorate a room which will then be photographed."

Big-Active
Good-value wallpaper

their dirodesi
ulation. There
sheriffs and c
remen too. And
the outmost sho
the pound of
the dacent ga
his pillowscone, t
his whirl wo
again? For hold
fidelios. They lai
bed. With a bock
feet. And a barrow
his head. Tee the toots
the twoddle of the fire

Hurrah, there is but young
globe for the ~~owl globe~~ wholly in view
which is ~~[illegible]~~ the same
thing. Well, Him a being so on the
~~flounder of his back~~ let wee peep
see, at Hom, well, see peegee ought he
ought? platterplate Ш. Hum! From Shopal
to beyond
and the head
to ireglint,
and all the

Graham Evans
Garbled wallpaper

A Fax is cheaper than phone or post provided you don't use complex imagery.

Fax is quicker.
Than what ? For what ? Why do we need to send things at the last minute?

A Fax communicates. So why do people phone up and say 'did you get my Fax?'
A Fax communicates to whom? Often not the right person.

A Fax is not private. It is very public.

Fax is an industry. It gives people jobs. It is also a consumption industry. More paper, more 'white boxes' to become redundant, crushed on the scrap heap after [illegible] the Design Museum archives.

You have to have a Fax machine in order to send or receive a Fax.

Fax transmits words and images. Words as text are more credible and authoritative than spoken words. They are accurate. Images are read more quickly than words. Images are becoming more important in communication. Think of all those illustrative corporate IDs. But the Fax can distort, condense and reduce the image so that it becomes almost unrecognisable. The image is grey, not in colour yet. The message has become distorted too.

You can produce a long continuous sheet on a Fax, just like you can on an image writer, or they did in Egypt on a papyrus roll, or in Victorian times on a pianola roll. So what ? Do we really need more metromania?

The high-tec Fax is encouraging low technology - handwriting. No not handwriting, not calligraphy, not italic, but just a speedy scrawl on the face sheet under 'comments'. A visual conversation without the art.

When you send a Fax, you don't pay for the paper, someone else pays for the paper. They pay for the paper. More paper.

When you send a Fax you get a receipt with the hour, minute, second and day when you sent it. It says O.K., or interrupt. It does not tell you that the people the other end received it. Or that the right individual person got it.

You can send the same mailshot Fax to lots and lots of different people throughout the world. [illegible]

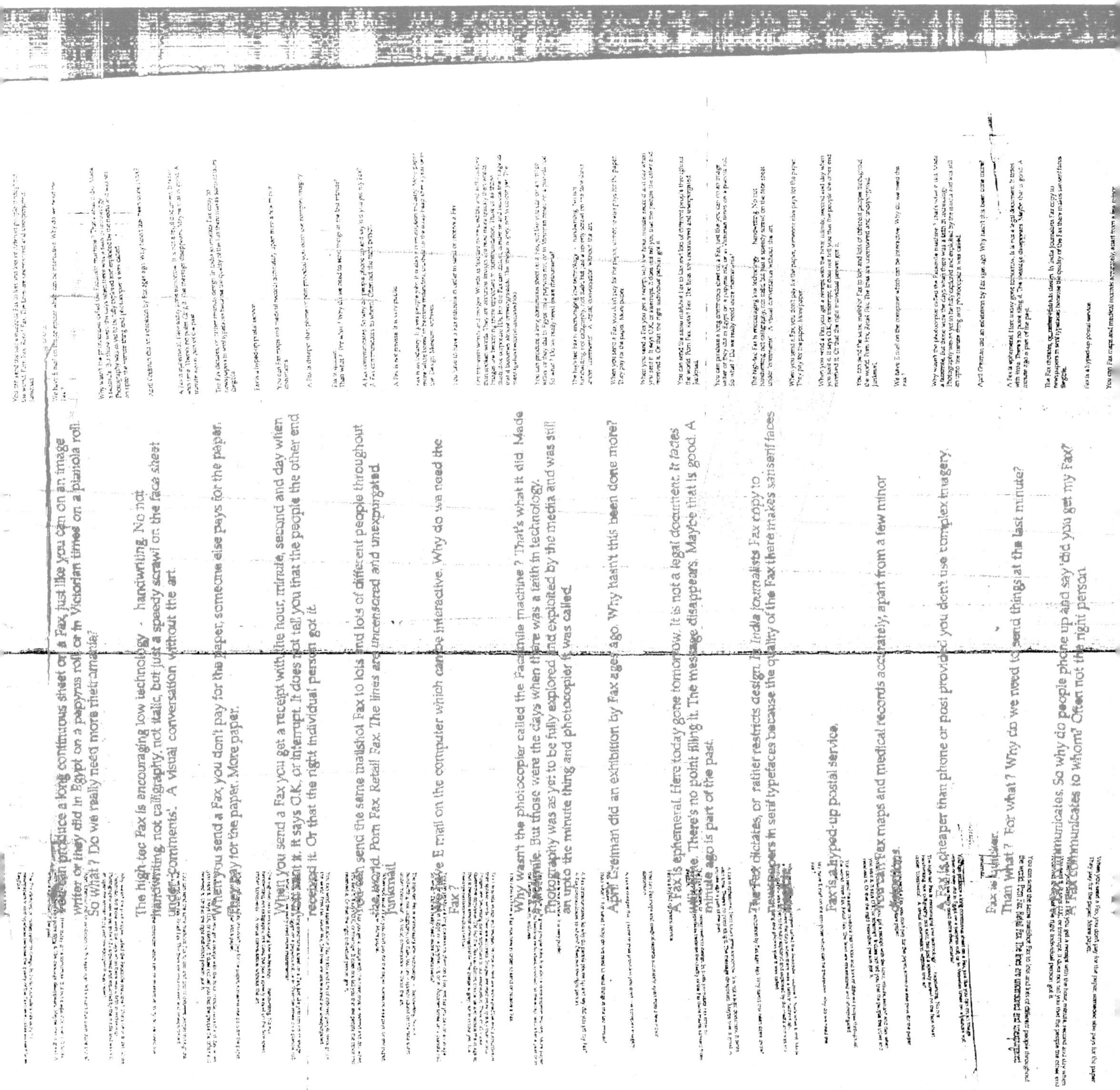

You can produce a long continuous sheet on a Fax, just like you can on an image writer or they did in Egypt on a papyrus roll or in Victorian times on a pianola roll. So what ? Do we really need more metromania?

The high-tec Fax is encouraging low technology - handwriting. No not handwriting, not calligraphy, not italic, but just a speedy scrawl on the face sheet under 'comments'. A visual conversation without the art.

When you send a Fax, you don't pay for the paper, someone else pays for the paper. They pay for the paper. More paper.

When you send a Fax you get a receipt with the hour, minute, second and day when you sent it. It says O.K. or interrupt. It does not tell you that the people the other end received it. Or that the right individual person got it.

You can send the same mailshot Fax to lots and lots of different people throughout the world. Porn Fax. Retail Fax. The lines are uncensored and unexpurgated. Junkmail.

We have E mail on the computer which can be interactive. Why do we need the Fax ?

Why wasn't the photocopier called the Facsimile machine ? That's what it did. Made a facsimile. But those were the days when there was a faith in technology. Photography was as yet to be fully explored and exploited by the media and was still an upto the minute thing and photocopier it was called.

April Greiman did an exhibition by Fax ages ago. Why hasn't this been done more?

A Fax is ephemeral. Here today gone tomorrow. It is not a legal document. It fades with time. There's no point filing it. The message disappears. Maybe that is good. A minute ago is part of the past.

The Fax dictates, or rather restricts design. In India journalists Fax copy to newspapers in serif typefaces because the quality of the Fax there makes sanserif faces illegible.

Fax is a hyped-up postal service.

You can Fax maps and medical records accurately, apart from a few minor distortions.

A Fax is cheaper than phone or post provided you don't use complex imagery.

Fax is quicker.
Than what ? For what ? Why do we need to send things at the last minute?

A Fax communicates. So why do people phone up and say 'did you get my Fax?'
A Fax communicates to whom? Often not the right person.

Bridget Wilkins
Fax/statements/
wallpaper

Angus Hyland
lufthansa Wallpaper

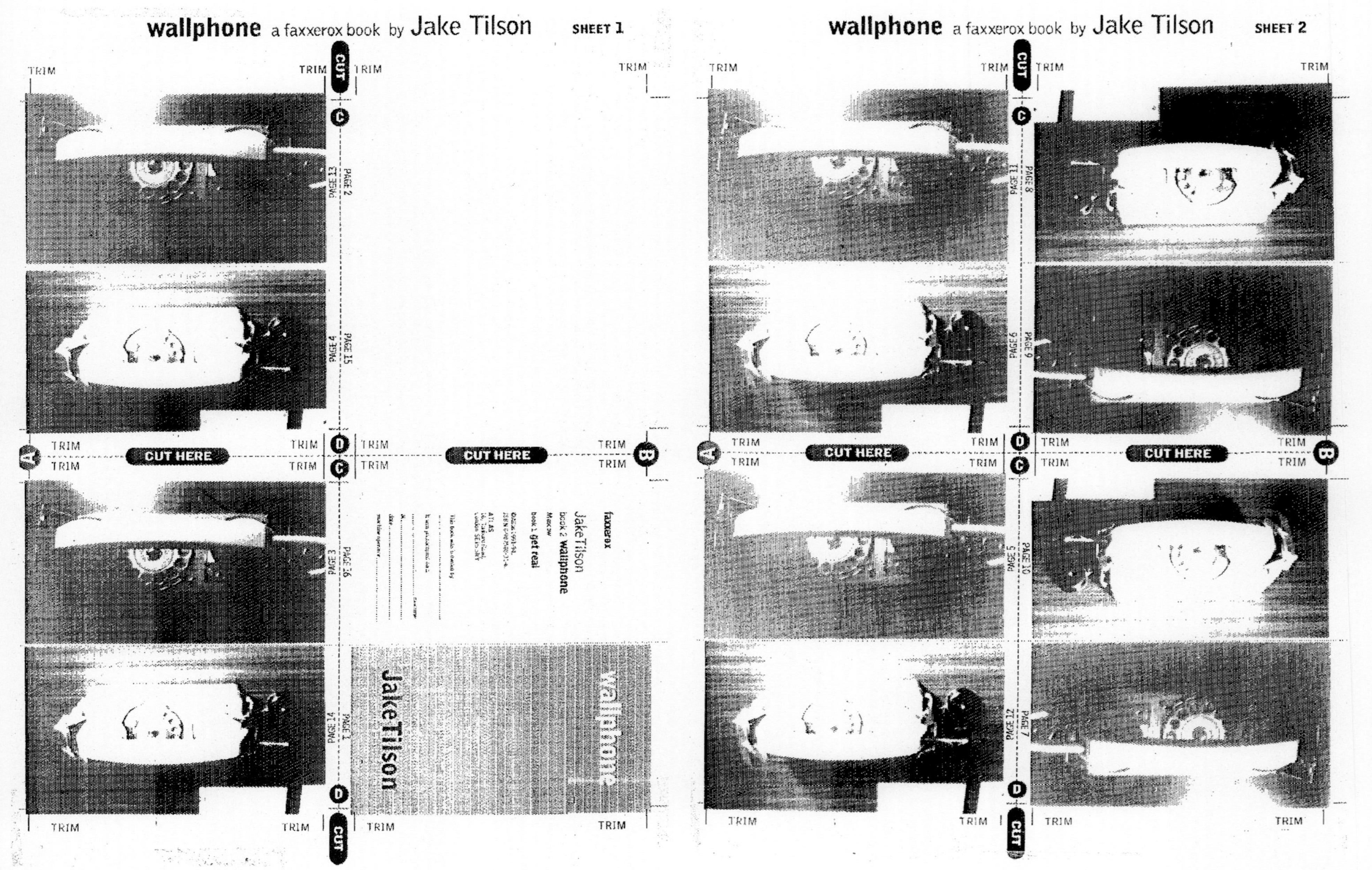

wallphone a faxxerox book by Jake Tilson
SHEET 1
wallphone a faxxerox book by Jake Tilson
SHEET 2
TRIM
CUT
CUT HERE
PAGE 13
PAGE 2
PAGE 4
PAGE 15
PAGE 3
PAGE 16
PAGE 14
PAGE 1
faxxerox
Jake Tilson
book 2 wallphone
book 1 get real
wallphone
Jake Tilson
PAGE 11
PAGE 8
PAGE 6
PAGE 9
PAGE 5
PAGE 10
PAGE 12
PAGE 7

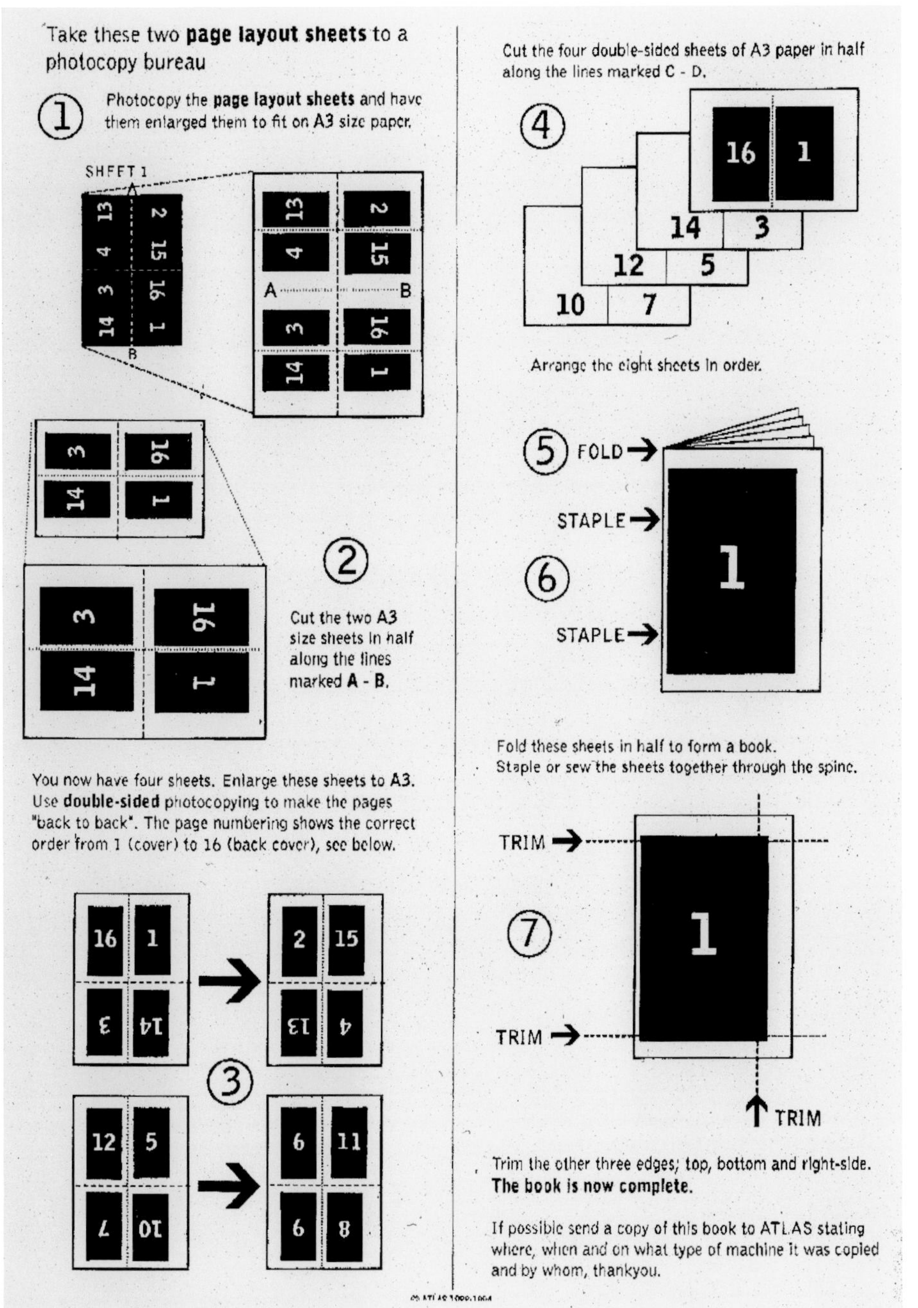
Take these two **page layout sheets** to a photocopy bureau
① Photocopy the **page layout sheets** and have them enlarged them to fit on A3 size paper.
SHEET 1
A
B
② Cut the two A3 size sheets in half along the lines marked **A - B**.
You now have four sheets. Enlarge these sheets to A3. Use **double-sided** photocopying to make the pages "back to back". The page numbering shows the correct order from 1 (cover) to 16 (back cover), see below.
③
Cut the four double-sided sheets of A3 paper in half along the lines marked C - D.
④
Arrange the eight sheets in order.
⑤ FOLD
STAPLE
⑥
STAPLE
Fold these sheets in half to form a book.
Staple or sew the sheets together through the spine.
TRIM
⑦
TRIM
TRIM
Trim the other three edges; top, bottom and right-side.
The book is now complete.
If possible send a copy of this book to ATLAS stating where, when and on what type of machine it was copied and by whom, thankyou.

ID
Jake Tilson

+44 71 701 3689

date
1994 02 20

duration
00 02' 59"

"Fax xerox" is an idea I had in 1991 when I produced the first in this series called "Get Real" which was also meant to be published in a magazine/book and then photocopied to produce books. "Wallphone" has been made exclusively for Urgent Images."

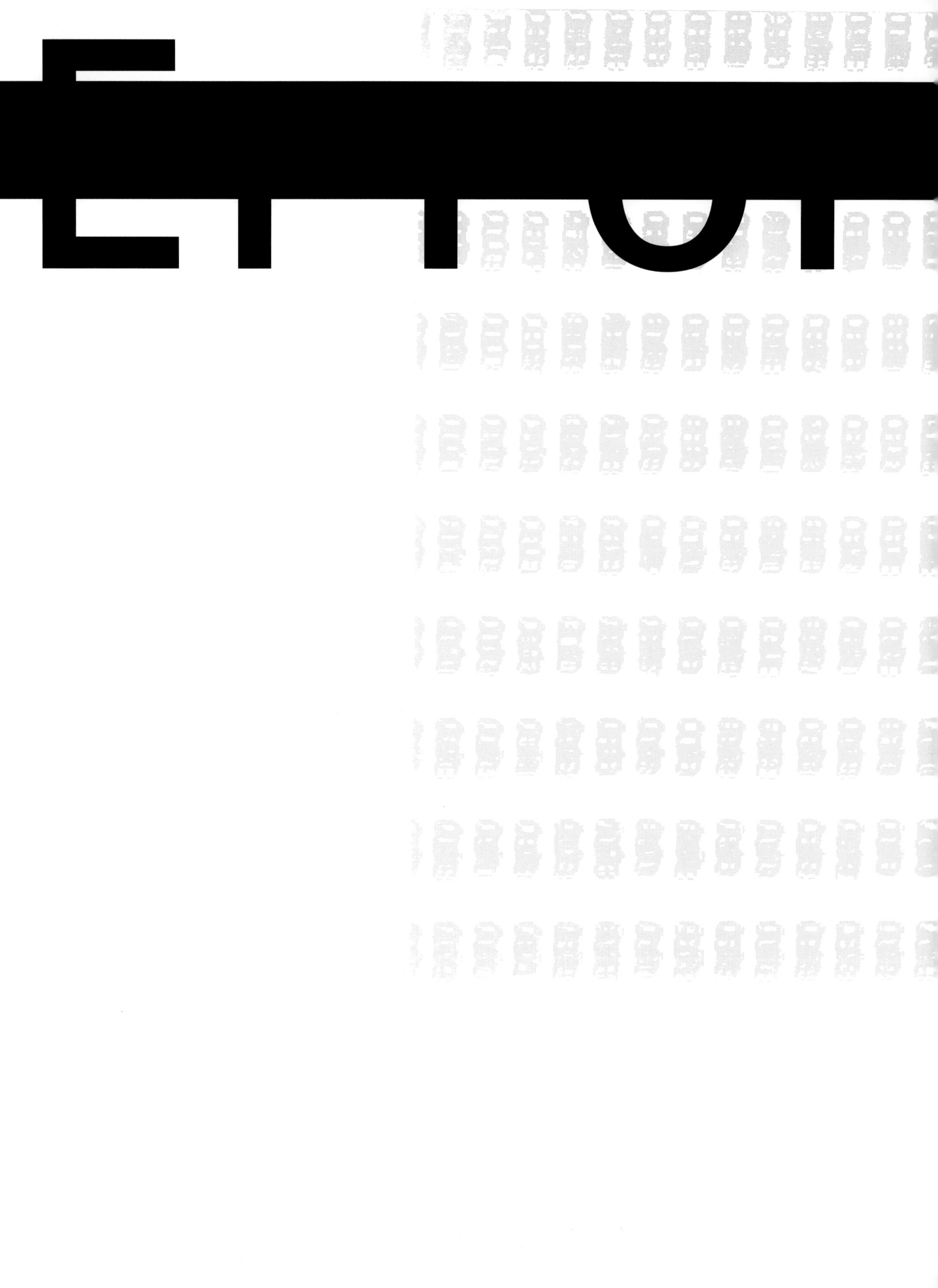

and space, a house,
a airport, a sigh

u side

a place on the sea

O cean

fox

DA :

Pagy Mc Queen 9-05-1994 7:35

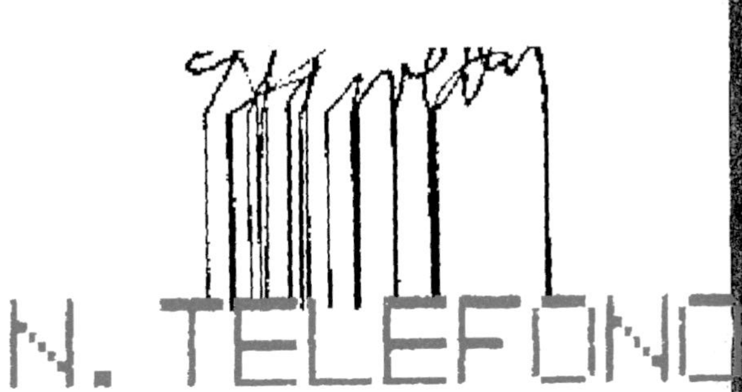
N. TELEFONO :

TRASMISSIONE INTERROTTA

A Fax is ephe ral. Here today gone tomorrow. It is not a legal document. It fades
with time.
minute ago is art of the past. The message disappears. Maybe that is good. A
The Fax

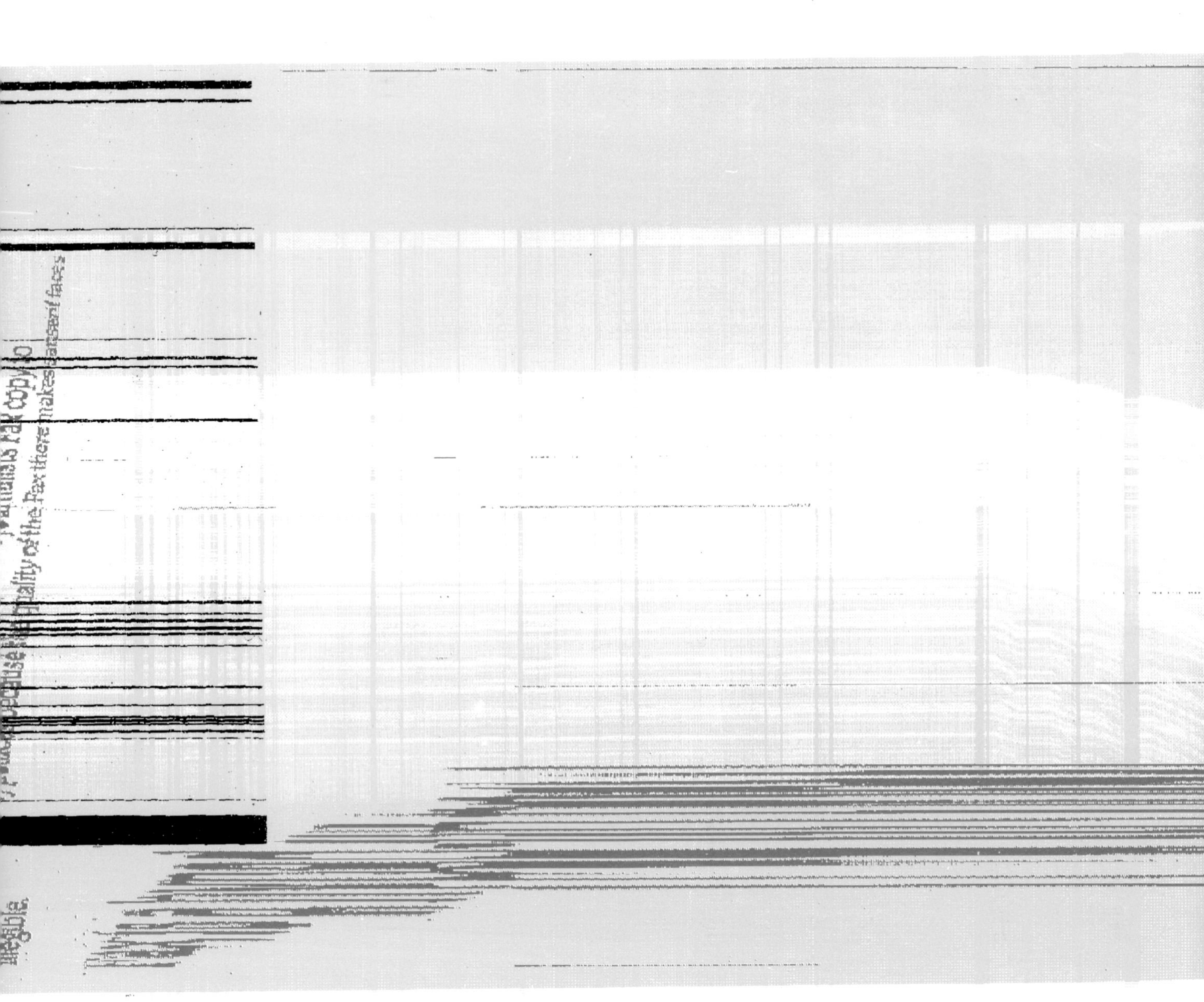

Termi

y

nolog

Activity report
A printout of fax numbers called stating dates, times and durations.

ADF/Automatic document feeder
Stack up to 50 sheets of paper, press "send" and walk away.

Analogue
Method of representing a transmission by electrical signals which directly relate to the scanned original.

Broadcast
Sending one document to many destinations automatically dialled from the memory.

Copy mode
You may use your fax machine as a photocopier.

Data compression
Omits "redundant" information in order to increase transmission capability.

Delayed memory send
Scan a document into the memory to be sent at off-peak rates.

Digital
Method of representing material to be transmitted as encoded binary information. Digital encodement is computer compatible.

Dual access
The ability to receive faxes while sending.

Duration/transmission time
The time it takes to send a fax.

ECM/Error correction mode
Accuracy of a transmission is verified, and if an error occurred the fax is automatically resent.

Grey scale
Halftones are reproduced in approximate, fixed shades of grey, up to 64 depending on the specifications of the sender's and receiver's machines.

Handshake
The initial contact between two machines, which checks compatibility and sets the mode (automatic or manual) and speed of transmission. Perceived as singing tones.

Header
Programmable information printed out at the top of a fax; user's name, number, date, duration etc. These have been elaborated into cover-sheets or "fax headers".

Huffman code
How images are encoded for transmission. In its "modified" mode it cuts out redundant horizontals from the image, transmitting them as white space.

Memory
From Group 3 up, most fax machines have a memory capability which facilitates storage of a fax for transmission when telephone lines are quieter and cheaper.

Modified (modified) read code
Depending on the level of modification, cuts out redundant verticals, as well as horizontals, from images thereby reducing transmission time on-line. Only applies to models produced by certain manufacturers.

One-touch dialling
Store a number in the memory and hit one button to dial.

On-line
Time spent connected to another fax machine.

Polling
Calls numbers from memory and requests other machines send their stored faxes.

Resolution
As with other printing methods dpi/dots per inch denotes the quality of the printed image. Fax machines offer the option of fine and extra fine modes which increase the dpi.

Smoothing
Extra dots are added to letter forms to counteract the jagged edges caused by bit-mapping and low dpi.

UHQ/Ultra high quality photo mode
Again, exclusive to certain manufacturer's machines, this option enhances grey scale.

end of transmission
london saying taraaaaa